Surrealism

Surrealism/ by YVES DUPLESSIS

Translated by Paul Capon

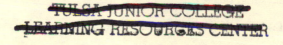

GREENWOOD PRESS, PUBLISHERS
WESTPORT, CONNECTICUT

Library of Congress Cataloging in Publication Data

Duplessis, Yves, 1912-
    Surrealism.

    Translation of Surréalisme.
    Reprint of the ed. published by Walker, New York in
series: A Sun book.
    1. Surrealism. 2. Arts, Modern--20th century.
I. Title.
[NX600.S9D8413 1978]   700'.9'04   77-17880
ISBN 0-313-20110-2

First published in France as *Le Surréalisme*. © 1950, Presses
Universitaires de France.

Reprinted with the permission of Walker and Company

Reprinted in 1978 by Greenwood Press, Inc.
51 Riverside Avenue, Westport, CT 06880

Printed in the United States of America

Preface

Surrealism is often thought of as intellectual snobbism, or as spiritual decadence, or simply as a joke played by artists eager to astonish at any cost. So easy is it to hurl anathema at innovators who, as they struggle to pursue their spiritual adventures, are driven beyond the confines of established prejudices. Yet the Surrealists' aim is extraliterary, since their aspiration is nothing less than to free man from the constraints of a too-utilitarian civilization, to shake him from his torpor, and to do this they have had to stress everything that can disconcert him. A deliberate turning away from intelligence has been necessary, and a rediscovery of the nature of the vital forces, so that their turbulent energies may carry man toward an infinitely widened horizon.

The recovery of those unrealized energies was the first step to be undertaken, since Surrealism (according to André Breton) rested in the philosophical sense "on a belief in the superior reality of certain hitherto neglected forms of association, those occurring in the dream's omnipotence and in the unfettered play of thought." The surrender to automatic thought patterns could alone allow this descent toward the province of the instincts and of repressed desires, which is the province of Surreality.

Yet, as art is the best medium for expressing this flood of deep psychological states, the works produced tend to be judged only from the aesthetic point of view, when in fact they are nothing less than glimpses into our most intimate self. Also, the leader of Surrealism insists unendingly that the poet must return to the surface after indulging the transports of his imagination, so that his personality can be enriched by the prizes gained during his plunges. Thus, the Surrealists use the discoveries of Freud, who, by rationalizing the subconscious, dealt a mortal blow to the spiritualistic beliefs in occult communications, and to the myth of escape into a supernatural universe. Several of André Breton's works show that happenings attributed to chance or adversity merely express the dynamism of instincts inhibited by social conventions. This is how Surreality connects with reality to indicate factually the synthesis of the sub-real and the real.

Although psychoanalysis allows the Surrealists to interpret the products of their experiments, they nevertheless want to go much further. It is not enough merely to show man his internal riches, he must also be given the power to employ them. The individual revolt of the spirit must be exchanged for an effective act of social upheaval. Psychoanalysis is complemented by Marxism, which destroys the obstacles standing in the way of the individual's free expansion. The individual must no longer divide himself into two hostile camps, and his actions must be encouraged to harmonize with his deepest inclinations. Surreality, in becoming the synthesis of theory and practice, enriches itself anew.

Far from taking refuge in ivory towers, the Surrealists aim only to demolish them—by the transformation of human existence—until reality's victims need no longer struggle to flee from reality, but, instead, may influence it, and make it conform to their aspirations. Moreover, just as the Surrealist movement has from the outset opposed the whole concept of art for art's sake, so will it reject the whole doctrine of revolution for revolution's sake, rejecting as well those who embrace one or the other of these misbegotten conceptions.

The notion of Surrealism has evolved deviously, but its different values converge toward a central theme: the realization of the integrated man. Humor will open the door to this goal, technology will provide the materials, art will be its language, psychoanalysis will give it its deep significance, and revolution will make possible its effective achievement.

Contents

Historical Introduction

From Romanticism evolved a movement that gradually came to scorn intelligible sense in a poem in preference for the apocalyptic obscurity of another universe. Of this movement Surrealism is a manifestation. At the very start of this era, poets such as Alfred de Vigny sought to give a philosophical content to their works and, according to Baudelaire, Victor Hugo's merit consisted in suggesting "the whole mystery of life."

In his turn, Baudelaire—the poet of hidden communication—expressed the unity of nature, "where sense, color, and sound all respond to each other." To a virtuous austerity he preferred escape from the world's limiting boundaries into the "artificial Paradises" of drunkenness— he who had so clear an understanding of human ambivalence.

Rimbaud, tragically living out his soul's conflict, at once in love with the absolute and a prisoner of the earthly hell, was profoundly influenced by Baudelaire, and in his life as in his work, he displayed his subjection to the headiness of the infinite. According to André Breton, "Rimbaud has done no more than express, with amazing vigor, a confusion encountered, no doubt, by many thousands of generations. Before he came, it was only at the rarest of intervals that we might stumble on, in a sage's lamentations, a philosopher's musing, or a criminal's confession, some understanding of this appalling duality that is the marvelous wound on which he has put his finger." Periods of disorder cast up these modern prophets who speak as poets, and in this sense Rimbaud was a forerunner of the Surrealists, a rebel against the human condition. He led the incoherent life of one who refuses to compromise with the social hypocrisies, and by his poems he endeavored to wrench men from themselves, showing them the ugliness of the accustomed scene. His work led toward an undiscovered world, that of the *Illuminations*, with their "objective visions."

The abysses of evil are bottomless, and their exploration brings a man all the intoxication of freedom, and a conviction of power that makes him exalt himself before God. Lautréamont, that other ancestor of Surrealism, has also lauded this revolt of the spirit, capable of carrying us into a world of terror and violence where the demoniac fantasy of Maldoror is freed of all shackles.

THUS, in the last years of the nineteenth century, "the idea, which is the poet's stock in trade" became a means of penetrating the mystery of a "super-nature" and enriched itself in a mystique that springs from the Rimbaudian revolt. At the same time, in numerous other spheres of thought, men were encouraged to remodel the conceptions that were keeping rationalism in check. The world, hitherto envisioned as a static concept, was now seen as part of a universal dynamism.

Indeed, Bergson, throughout his work, expounds the limitation of the intelligence, which can only function in the province of matter, whereas intuition allows us access to the very source of being. Anticipating Freud, this philosopher drew attention to the dream, as well as to the phenomena of telepathy and to various antirational manifestations in related fields.

In the same period a number of works were published that treated of mental sicknesses and their influence on character and development. Behavior was shown to be logical only superficially, and thus a novelist could bring the analysis of a philosophy to its conclusion by dissecting his characters' motives and showing that their conditioned conduct often concealed a fundamental absurdity. This explains the immediacy of Dostoievsky, for whom everyone's consciousness was the habitat of contradictory and irreconcilable tendencies.

Psychology was not alone in being disturbed by these revelations; the physical sciences were just as disconcerted by the discovery of the world of discontinuity, a world where indeterminism reigns. To literature was destined to fall the task of revealing the unity of the individual behind the confusion of his masks, and similarly, in painting, movements such as Cubism were to bring about the virtual dislocation of reality by thrusting beyond appearances to reach the very essence of people and things.

Guillaume Apollinaire, above all, compelled himself to aim at the unexpected, as his poems evince. In *Zone*, unrelated images mingle and follow one another, unendingly, just as in life they stream through our minds below the level of consciousness. It is Apollinaire also who "thinks with some reason that certain clichés such as 'coral lips'— the occurrence of which can be taken as a test of value —are the product of this activity qualified as *Surrealist*."

IN URGING ON still further this tendency toward disorientation, some people displayed in their very existences "this desire for the unexpected, typical of modern taste." Already Alfred Jarry had created his character Ubu, and Jarry's life was nothing less than a constant provocation of all bourgeois values.

After the armistice, Jacques Vaché, who, according to André Breton, was "a master of the art of attaching extremely little importance to anything," committed suicide in a quite mysterious fashion. A forerunner of Dadaism,

Vaché claimed the virtue of writing nothing at all because "to the foot of every work of art is chained this cannon-ball that holds down the soul after death." His influence on Breton as the promoter of Surrealism was decisive because "without him," Breton asserted, "I should perhaps have been a poet. However, for me, he frustrated that conspiracy of obscure tendencies that leads to a belief in something as absurd as a vocation."

Humor, as a destroyer of society, was displayed in an even more audacious way in the life of Arthur Cravan. A boxer by profession and a deserter in a number of countries, he created scandal wherever he went. Between 1912 and 1915 he brought out a review called *Maintenant,* selling copies of it from a costermonger's barrow that he pushed through the streets himself as a gesture of derision to the traditional and neglected bookshops. In its pages he violently criticized the painters, to whom he preferred the heroes of sport, who at least expressed in all their vitality the primitive instincts of the individual.

The search for a new conception of art instigated reviews such as *Sic,* which appeared in 1916 under the direction of Pierre-Albert Birot. Here again were found the tendencies of Futurism: the praise of machinery and of the cities' staccato rhythms. The next year, Pierre Reverdy—who among all living poets is the one who seems to André Breton "to have assumed, in the highest degree, the impetus so missing in Apollinaire"—founded *Nord-Sud.* But he made the error of taking refuge in "a purely static and contemplative attitude, which, by itself, is not enough." Collaborating with Reverdy in this review were Apollinaire, Max Jacob, and Louis Aragon.

Above all, it was *Literature*—the ironic title of a publication as antiliterary as conceivable—that posed the question of the movement's destination, which was inherent in all these probings toward a new reality. In its earliest numbers, its directors, André Breton, Philippe Soupault, and Louis Aragon, conducted an inquiry—entitled "Why Do You Write?"—that indicated sharply how vain the anxieties of aesthetic opinion seemed to them, when there were problems as weighty as the future of human existence to be solved. The very act of writing implies a concession, it is an act of compromise, so what is the good of writing?

This contempt for art, this intellectual nihilism affecting young people haunted by the search for the absolute, was also to be found in America, where as early as 1912 Marcel Duchamp had gone so far as to sign his name to ready-made objects such as bicycle wheels and portmanteaux. Francis Picabia, who brought the news of this to France, likewise displayed "a wonderful detachment from everything." When he arrived in Zurich, he at once attached himself to the Dada movement, the creator of which, Tristan Tzara, was not to arrive in Paris until 1919. There Picabia sought to rally all those striving to smash the established routines: Philippe Soupault, then the *Literature* group, together with Pierre Reverdy and Jean Cocteau.

DADAISM is the spiritual terminus of those made desperate by the destruction of their fellow men and of the world, of those who can no longer believe in stability or the permanent. It was in a Zurich café in 1916 that Tristan Tzara invented the word "Dada," and the very insignificance of its two syllables was a spur to his circle's enthusiasm. The Dadaists deeply deplored the agony and lack of balance that they knew would follow the war, and their movement was the search for a formula to live by. Not only their works but their very existence was Dada, that is, a constant revolt directed as much against art as against morality and society. The Dadaists wanted to scandalize opinion and to shake it from its lethargy. "To avoid falling back into the habits hallowed and made natural by a long tradition, they insisted on all that was baroque, off-balance, and unexpected, so that the fine, the noble, and the exalted would not be permitted to grow the fur of the beast." This was the explanation of one of them: Georges Ribémont-Dessaignes.

By its nature this movement escaped the common aesthetic qualifications, because the rebels were too aware of the vanity of earthly things. To avoid being classified they strove above all to reject all that by tradition was expected of avant-garde movements, and the public, seeking to judge their emergence on an artistic plane, was indignant when one of them, Tristan Tzara, instead of the announced manifesto, read an article picked at random from a magazine, while Paul Eluard and Theodore Fraenkel tapped out an accompaniment on bells. According to Jacques Rivière, the Dadaists "vowed to realize without choice, without object, and without predilection, every facet of their spirit. They offered up this universal transmutability that is the power at the heart of each of us, and that can be subdued only by meditation and the will." All scales of value are suppressed, all distinction between what should be done or not done, said or not said, is abolished; it is enough to make actual "exactly and at all times what passes through your head, so that the spirit is held in a state of original selection [*ballottage originel*]."

Benjamin Peret and Jacques Rigaud joined the Dadaist movement in 1920, and on May 26 of that year its last manifestation took place, since it was inherent in Dada's position that it should end by destroying itself. But by freeing the spirit from its prejudices, it had opened the way for a positive movement—Surrealism.

The fervid behavior of the Dadaists, their endless insults to society, their contempt for conventions, all demonstrated their desire to free man from the hypocrisy that held him enslaved. André Breton, unable to resign himself to such a negative position, cried: "I take care to adapt my life to the derisory conditions of all human existence." The intention was to attain, in all possible ways, the "human form entirely restored," superseding experience based on "expediency" and "it's only sound sense." Dada having destroyed the traditional idea of classical man, it now fell to the Surrealists to create a new one. That is to say, skepticism was to contribute both to the destruction of an outdated order and to the preparation of a regenerated humanity.

Thus 1921 saw the end of Dada, the effigy of which was thrown into the Seine, as had been the effigies of Cubism and of Futurism, by the students of the Quatz'Arts School.

A METHODICAL INVESTIGATION of the Surreal took the place of scandal and rebellion. André Breton, supported by Louis Aragon, Paul Eluard, Max Ernst, Pierre de Massot, Max Morise, Pierre Unik, and Roger Vitrac, became the leader of this movement, which started by exploring the unconscious. *Les Champs Magnétiques*, written by André Breton and Philippe Soupault, appeared in 1921, and from 1922 to 1924 they again put out the results of their researches, in the review *Literature*. To them rallied Maxime Alexandre, Antonin Artaud, Joseph Delteil, Francis Gerard, André Masson, Pierre Naville, and Max Noll.

André Breton soon expelled from his group those disciples who let themselves be tempted by literary glory or politics, since Surrealist activity is essentially uncommitted. As the defender of its purity he next eliminated "those who, in certain respects more or less obvious, have not deserved freedom." Thus he soon parted company with Jean Cocteau, Jean Paulhan, Raymond Radiguet, Jules Romains, André Salmon, and Paul Valéry, on account of the large editions of their works. Chirico, and then in 1936, Salvador Dali, both guilty of being converts to fascism, and Joseph Delteil, due to his conversion to Catholicism, were excluded in their turn.

In 1924 André Breton published the *Premier Manifeste du Surréalisme;* the "Bureau de Recherches Surréalistes" was founded at 15, rue de Grenelle; and, on December 1, the first number of the *Révolution Surréaliste* appeared, under the control of Pierre Naville and Benjamin Peret. This review, which was published until 1929, had an experimental aspect. In it were found accounts of dreams, automatic texts, replies to inquiries on suicide and love, and attacks upon Anatole France and Paul Claudel that clearly demonstrated its revolutionary tendencies.

Although at the time of the war in Morocco, the Surrealists, taking the Communists' part, stirred up various scandals, André Breton's enthusiasm was particularly roused by Trotsky, and by a communism that he considered humanistic enough for the period. As always his political sympathies never led him to total adherence; a true artist has too much need of his independence. Moreover, toward the end of 1925, following a lively bout of polemics, Breton broke with Pierre Naville, who maintained that intellectual life depended entirely upon social conditions and who withdrew to dedicate himself to the control of *Clarté,* a Communist conformist review.

The *Second Manifeste du Surréalisme* appeared in

1929, and in it André Breton stated his exact political position. In its pages he censured several more of his disciples, such as Antonin Artaud, who, he maintained, had acted ostentatiously in wanting to stage Strindberg's *The Dream* before the Swedish ambassador. He parted company also with such founders of the movement as Philippe Soupault, whose orientation had become too literary, and Robert Desnos, who, absorbed by automatic writing, had lost interest in concrete problems. Still with him at this period, as pure representatives of Surrealism, were Louis Aragon, Paul Eluard, and Pierre Unik.

One magazine, *Grand Jeu,* founded by Roger-Gilbert Lecomte, Rolland de Reneville, and René Daumal, envisaged Surrealism with esoteric and mystical aspects as foreshadowed by Rimbaud, but served only to create further dissension. For André Breton, the point was not to escape into a supernatural world, but to accomplish something positive in this one. His ambition was to influence facts in a practical manner while at the same time pursuing his investigations into the intellect's internal activities, as was testified in *L'Immaculée Conception,* written in collaboration with Paul Eluard, and published in 1930.

When the ex-members of Surrealism tried to bury the movement—in a pamphlet entitled *Un Cadavre*—the interment proved to be premature, since at that moment André Breton was gathering about him a new host of poets, such as Luis Bunuel, René Char, and Georges Hugnet; and of painters, such as Salvador Dali and Yves Tanguy. Already, in 1928, he had analyzed the qualities of several of the latter in his book *Le Surréalisme et la Peinture.*

Meanwhile he pursued his revolutionary activities, and his review took on the title of *Surréalisme au Service de la Révolution,* continuing to appear until 1933. Its appeals for revolution appeared side by side with Salvador Dali's expositions of a method he had discovered for exploring the unconscious.

However, a new conflict sprang into being when Louis Aragon returned from the Kharkov congress of 1930 completely converted to Soviet Communism. This exploded into a separation from André Breton. It was Breton's same Trotskyite sympathies that, in 1938, caused him to expel Paul Eluard and Georges Hugnet.

In 1935, in his *Position Politique du Surréalisme,* he upheld the independence of the artist in his relation to society. At this time, too, the Surrealists were collaborating in an art review, *Minotaure.* It contained inquiries into various subjects, some automatic texts by a fourteen-year-old girl, Gisele Prassinos, and, above all, reproductions of a number of Surrealist pictures by Salvador Dali, Max Ernst, Yves Tanguy, Hans Arp, Alberto Giacometti, René Magritte, Man Ray, and Joan Miro.

Far from dying, Surrealism was extending itself and spreading abroad. An exhibition was held in London in 1936, and André Breton convened conferences in Central Europe, Switzerland, and the Canary Islands. Another Surrealist manifesto was published in Paris in 1938, and in the same year André Breton went to Mexico to meet Leon Trotsky. Once more Trotsky asserted their spiritual harmony, and on Breton's return to France he published an article in *Minotaure* in which he raised his voice afresh against "nationalism in art."

Then came the war. Salvador Dali and Yves Tanguy left for the United States. Benjamin Peret remained in Paris until 1941, then went to Mexico; and after once more taking up his profession of doctor, André Breton, followed by André Masson, went to America to continue his researches independently. In New York in 1942 he published *Les Prolégomènes à un Troisième Manifeste du Surréalisme ou Non*, then *Arcane 17*. In May, 1946, he returned to Paris, where, in the course of an interview, he confirmed the intransigence of his position. More than ever, he said, in a period thrown out of kilter by the rebirth of material appetites, the pursuit of the ideal imposed itself as a duty.

In the atomic age man ought to react against all ready-made concepts and should do everything possible to bring about the advent of a new human era. Already the lowering of standards was so great that even a Surrealist conformism was establishing itself. "In particular," said Breton, "too many paintings appear in the world today that have been produced at the cost of no sacrifice whatsoever to the innumerable followers of Chirico, Picasso, Ernst, Miro, Tanguy, etc." Then he amused himself by recalling that "in art there is no great enterprise undertaken except at the peril of one's life . . . , and every artist should venture upon nothing less than the pursuit of the Golden Fleece."

In America, just as in France, he continued, "the main part of poetic production" lacked the essential quality, which is "surprise." He added, "The accent should be put on the power to exceed, which is the function of *movement* and of *freedom.* In this respect Reverdy, Picabia, Peret, Artaud, Arp, Michaux, Prevert, Char, and Cesaire stand as so many inimitable models." And, in 1947, many visitors to the Surrealist exhibition held in Paris were disconcerted by a whole cycle of exhibits inspired by primitive magic.

The movement seemed then to be leading toward an occult knowledge of the universe. *Surrealist Communication* appeared from November, 1953, to January, 1955, as a new series under the name *Medium,* and in 1957 André Breton's *L'Art Magique* was published. It was always a question of encouraging "the search for a much greater liberation of the mind," and, according to a revue directed by André Breton since 1956, this searching is what Surrealism really is. Breton was at that time associated with Jean Schuster, Andre-Pieyre de Mandiargues, Charles Estienne, and Robert Benayoum. In Paris, "on the threshold of the year 1960," he organized, with the help of Marcel Duchamp, an International Exhibition of Surrealism, the theme of which was eroticism, "the only art that can keep pace with both man and the infinite, that can lead him beyond the stars."

Therefore, this movement, this spiritual flow, too often thought of as belonging to history, preserves its dynamism.

No doubt, in the face of Existentialism and of Marxism, it will have to state and defend its positions, but at all events its fertility can never be brought into question, venturing as it does into those strange provinces where alone we can start to experience the power and sway of poetry.

1 / Surrealist Techniques

Humor

The shabbiness and stupidity of this world—the arena of human existence—can only render it ridiculous or comical to him who aspires to the infinite. Before we can plan a new life, much must be demolished, and laughter is still the best tool for loosening hypocrisy's grip. Surely this power to free ourselves from the shackles and constraints of society is a privilege in itself and, while Satan leads the dance, the Surrealists hoot their derision from the depths of the subconscious.

The humorist detaches himself from life so that he can consider it as a spectator. Before his gaze perform the puppets, of which he has only to see the strings to realize the illusory seriousness of their comportment and the superficiality of their gravity. Real life loses its earnestness and becomes a subject for flippancy as soon as we can regard it with indifference. Thus, humor implies detachment; it is the point of view of him who gazes upon the world's frenzy from his balcony.

Mockery of the conventions, and a stressing of the absurdities, must inevitably end in a revolt against established order. As Freud has shown, humor is an expression of insubordination, and a refusal to bow to the social prejudices; it is the disguise of the desperate.

Yet humor is more than the mark of a spirit refusing to be cowed by events, and in a more noble aspect it expresses the ego's will to free itself from reality to the point of indifference to its slings and arrows. The shocks of the outside world can even occasion pleasure. Freud, says André Breton, cites as an example the condemned man who was taken to the scaffold on a Monday and who cried "This is a fine start to the week!" By shielding us from "the expense inherent in suffering," humor has "an immensely valuable quality," and "we recognize it as especially appropriate for emancipating us and exalting us." Is it not humor that "Père Ubu" incarnates when he explodes "the whole assemblage of powers unknown, unconscious, and suppressed, of which the ego, totally kept under by prudence, is the only permitted emanation"?

This is why humor, the expression of revolt, is a moral attitude, as Marco Ristitch has pointed out in an article in the *Révolution Surréaliste*. "To understand the lamentable vanity of everything, its absurd unreality, is to understand your own uselessness—it is to be useless. Therefore, if you are to transcend negation, you must either completely annihilate yourself or completely transform yourself. Vaché has killed himself, Dada has become Surrealism. . . . Surrealism goes straight into the forbidden zone."

By giving us a different slant on the world, humor breaks up the familiar relationships of objects. It

> is essentially an implied and intuitive criticism of conventional thought patterns, a force that takes a fact, or a collection of facts, from what is considered a normal context, and throws it into a dazzling display of unexpected and superreal juxtapositions. By mixing reality and fantasy outside the limits of everyday realism and reasoned logic, humor, and humor alone, lends to its surroundings a grotesque newness and a hallucinatory quality of nonbeing . . . endowing its targets with a derisory importance linked to a sort of "super-sense" that, though special and ephemeral, is all-embracing. . . .

It turns our accustomed attitudes upside down by misplacement, surprise, and unexpected associations. It frees the spirit and gives it wings.

Rationalism itself rebels against this form of intellectual activity, which, as the *Chants de Maldoror* have best shown, is destructive to law, classification, and established order.

Poetry, which, like life itself, can present a succession of situations, lends itself better to humor than does painting. Nevertheless, when painting is thought of as a medium for the expression of internal dynamism, humorous works will be created, such as those of Max Ernst. Speaking of Ernst's three "novels" in collage, André Breton has said, "There is nothing more accomplished or exemplary than his *La Femme Sans Tête, Rêve d'une Petite Fille Qui Voulut Entrer au Carmel,* and *Une Semaine de Bonté ou Les Sept Eléments Capitaux.*"

It is, however, the cinema that has come to be humor's chosen territory. Its resources give the spirit's fancy a free run, as is shown in animated cartoons and in some American films that suggest a newborn reality in which, thanks to unexpected meetings of objects not normally associated, burlesque triumphs. Antonin Artaud, believing humor to be a means of freeing mankind's instinctive forces, looks upon an early film of the Marx Brothers, *Animal Crackers,* as an apocalypse. By means of the screen, this team achieves "an especial magic that the accepted relationships of words and images do not usually reveal, and if Surrealism can be described as a state characterized by a distinct and poetic degree of the spirit, then *Animal Crackers* entirely shares it." In speaking of the humor of this film and in evaluating it Artaud refers to "the idea of something disquieting and tragic, of a looming destiny (neither fortunate nor unfortunate, yet painful by definition) that insinuates itself like the symptom of an atrocious disease on an otherwise entirely beautiful face." Humor is more than just a corrosive satire of reality; it substitutes for reality a universe where everything is new for those who explore it.

DESTRUCTIVE HUMOR, aimed at life's everyday aspects, disconcerts the mind by the unexpected and, in detaching it from its usual attitudes, prepares it to glimpse another reality—Surreality. The Surrealists, unlike the Dadaists, are not content merely to wipe the slate clean—they also want to produce positive work. Once logic abases itself before imagination, a rich field of images and fantasy opens up. The Surrealists invite us to step beyond the utilitarian world where material gain is the prime motive, so that we can set foot in another world, altogether marvelous and mysterious. "Surrealism is the expression of our will for the total dissociation of everything from everything." Thus, a statue in a ditch has entirely different values from the same statue on its pedestal, and similarly, to isolate a hand from its arm alters its significance.

The thing is to detach objects from each other, to no longer consider them in any particular relationship, but as they are in themselves. Then we shall see that they are susceptible of many interpretations, proving the flimsiness of the values generally given them. Although this phase of physical misplacement was to lead the Existentialists to the concept of nothingness, in the hands of the Surrealists it produced a new philosophy of aesthetics. Max Ernst has explained to us why it is that beauty can, in Isidore Ducasse's formula, be born from "the meeting of a sewing machine and an umbrella on a dissecting table." That is to say:

A ready-made reality, the original purpose of which seems to be inherent in it and fixed for all times (an umbrella), finds itself in the presence of another reality quite remote in its purpose, and no less absurd (the sewing machine), and this in a place where either would be considered inappropriate (on a dissecting table). Given this situation, the umbrella escapes from its original purpose and its identity. It moves from its false absolute, via a relative, to a new absolute, and one that is true and poetic.

The attribution of a fictitious and disconcerting quality to familiar objects, says Louis Aragon, is not merely a game, but a philosophical attitude. In effect, the philosopher puts himself in the position of the crowd in order to attain a particular vision, one the world does not expect. "Common knowledge is established as a result of a stable relationship, accompanied by a judgment that assumes such abstractions as it can command; this judgment is reality." However,

> The concept of the real is foreign to all true philosophy. . . . Since the existence of the real is denied, philosophical knowledge has to extract from its materials a new arrangement, the unreal; and at once, the invention of this concept itself moves into the realm of the unreal. Then philosophy denies the existence of the unreal in its turn. It escapes. And this double negation, far from ending with the affirmation of the real, repels it, confounds it with the unreal, and surpasses both concepts to grasp a third, one in which they are

at once denied and affirmed, and which reconciles and contains them: the Surreal, which is one of the determinations of poetry.

A well-known parlor trick—the one where three matches are fixed to their box in the form of a portico so that lighting the middle of the crosswise one causes it to shoot away—is a philosophical act of the first magnitude. For, although we call this a trick, we have given the name "surreal usage" to the match that allows us to penetrate a new world where usefulness is not relevant. It is in such contrivances that "Surrealist humor exists in a natural state and without the least stage management."

Surrealism has, then, a double aspect, negative and positive. For a start, accepted reality must be destroyed so that from its enclosing shell a new reality can spring up. Then humor, by exerting criticism of the normal and logical relationships of objects, images, and words, precipitates them into another universe, taking them to the point where their identity can be put to the test, and finally, by means of unexpected visual shocks, the intellect can be made to return to a state of unprejudiced confusion.

ANDRÉ BRETON, exploring still further the philosophical significance of humor, finds in it a conception of knowledge. Since the Romantic era, two forces have competed for dominance in art: "that which persuades the interest to fasten itself on the fortunes of the external world" and that "which would have it concentrate upon the caprices of human personality." If they alternate, as with Lautréamont, they end "as in the case of Jarry, with the triumph of *objective humor,* which is their dialectical resolution. . . . Marcel Duchamp, Raymond Roussel, Jacques Vaché, Jacques Rigaud . . . even wanted to codify this sort of humor. The whole Futurist movement, and the whole Dadaist movement, can claim it as their essential factor."

Yet the aspect of humor that André Breton calls "*subjective*" and that arises from "the personality's need to attain its highest degree of independence" effaces itself more and more before its first component. In Apollinaire's case its demands led to obscurantism, once he "never stopped urgently pleading the case for automatism. The practice of psychic automatism, fundamental to Surrealism's progress, enlarged the field of the immediately fortuitous in all spheres, but—and this is the cardinal point—this fortuity, on examination, strongly denies being fortuitous at all."

That is to say, the irrational seems at first glance to result from chance and coincidence, and serves only to disturb the intellect. But the analysis of those fortuitous meetings of events and images shows that certain phenomena, such as telepathy, and even clairvoyance, arise from a necessity that man fails to understand, "even though the necessity vigorously asserts itself." Objective humor shatters against the sudden walls of this "unexplored region . . . where transcendental experiences await the spirit," and this is the region of *objective chance.*

Humor not only conducts us into a universe of the imagination, it also enables us to attain a philosophic concept of the world—a concept informed by "a rationality far larger than any other," which will unite both worlds, that of the dream and that of reality. This view of André Breton's accords with the discoveries of modern science, which discards the principle of determinism. Thus, the haughty pretensions of classic determinism, subjecting all phenomena to a rigorous foreordination, are swept away before a more fluid conception, since, in the microphysical world, we can never know with precision a molecule's position and speed at a given moment. Werner Heisenberg has gone so far as to speak of the "principle of uncertainty."

Science, however, goes further, and in a way that confirms a theory dear to André Breton—that the whole explanation of a phenomenon results from a fusion of objective and subjective factors. Illustrating this is the scientist's need to illuminate a molecule in order to observe it: the light-beam produces actions and reactions that modify the molecule's position and speed to an unknown degree. Is not this phenomenon analogous to the one in introspection, whereby, as Louis de Broglie has pointed out, the contemplation of a sentiment is often enough to modify its course? Thus science is far from being rigorously objective, because it is impossible to isolate the observer's personal reflexes. Physical actions and interactions become mixed with those arising from human psychology, and, as André Breton has written, "an over-rationalism, such as defines the philosopher's real position (resulting from the idea of a non-Euclidean geometry, followed by a generalized geometry, non-Newtonian mechanics, non-Maxwellian physics, etc.) cannot fail to correspond to an overt realism or Surrealism, which brings disaster upon the Cartesian-Kantian structure, and completely overthrows the idea of sensibility."

By different, and even opposite, paths, the artist and the philosopher end by meeting in a new and enlarged concept of the real, into which goes "all that can be held of the irrational subjected to a new rule."

The Marvelous

Thus Surrealism, by its assessment of reality, associates itself with the movement that has shaken the foundations of determinism in science, and has exposed the abstraction of the systems of pure logic in philosophy.

Anyone coming to that province where the grotesque and the mysterious shed their quality of strangeness discovers, with Paul Eluard, that "everything is comparable to everything else, everything has its echo, its likeness, and its opposite. Everything has its ubiquitous proliferation, and this proliferation is infinite." This idea of a universal mutability was already cherished by the German Romantics, and it suggested to Claude Estève, the heroine of André Breton's *Nadja*, "that in a previous existence Nadja could certainly have been Novalis, that poet of magical idealism for whom the most natural of attitudes was to see the marvelous in the commonplace and the usual, and who kept the strange and the supernatural like familiars at his elbow."

In this fantastic universe the most improbable happenings seem normal, the critical spirit is abolished, and constraints vanish. This enchanted world is truly that of Surreality. Already Isidore Ducasse and Arthur Rimbaud had opened "an entirely new avenue to poetry, and by systematically defying all the accustomed ways of reacting both to the world's spectacle and to themselves, they threw themselves headlong into the marvelous."

As Louis Aragon has written, "There are other truths than the real that the spirit can seize, and that are also primary, such as chance, illusion, the fantastic, and the dream. These various elements are united and reconciled in a manner that is Surreality." In his works, such as *Le Paysan de Paris,* he reveals this halo that surrounds the most everyday objects, this strange light that penetrates to the extraordinary. This ambiguous quality transforms, by means of the magic of his style, the shops in the passage of the Opéra. In the turmoil of such places he half-opens the locks that close no more than insecurely on the infinite. The strangeness of certain districts is like a second face, and the face that seems the more obvious turns out to be the more shallow. Yet sensitivity to the marvelous is a delicate and precious gift, which it is necessary to safeguard, since it "is lost upon any man who presses forward in his own life as along a road that is better and better paved, who advances in worldliness with ever-increasing ease, and who progressively rids himself of the taste for the unusual."

The Surrealists repudiate the real world so that they can venture into the world of phantoms and apparitions, since "it is only when the fantastic is approached to the point where human intellect loses command that the being's deepest emotions have every chance of manifesting themselves."

Antonin Artaud, fascinated by this endless interplay of magic and sorcery in real life, translated Matthew Lewis's *The Monk*. This book, according to André Breton, shows the passion for eternity of heroes freed from all earthly constraint and exalts "only that which inspires the spirit to leave the mundane."

Moreover, certain places favor flights of the imagination and, to state the Surrealist point of view, this involves "the matter of the chateaux." Lewis did not write *The Monk* until he had lived for a long time in an ancient mansion, Huysmans' novel *En Rade* came to him in a deserted castle, and André Breton, in *La Revolver à Cheveux Blancs*, describes a dream chateau. And has not Julien Gracq more recently called one of his novels *Au Chateau d'Argol?*

Surreality shows itself wherever the imagination can develop freely, without the restraint of the critical spirit. And for Pierre-Albert Birot "the marvelous, as it is freed more and more from fetters, takes the role of surprising reality in itself, and this is the role of Surrealism. . . . The marvelous performs the miracle of blending itself with the ordinary and commonplace in the most natural way in the world." If some people see this exalted prospect of the universe, others, in dream states and under the influence of ecstasy, make us perceive its profundity, and it is this profundity that Surrealism wants to reach and express. We must extricate ourselves from all the illusions that mask the Surreal world. If only, as André Breton has written, "we were rid of these famous trees, and of the houses, volcanoes, and empires. . . . Surrealism's secret rests in the fact that we are persuaded that something is hidden behind them."

The Dream

As a forerunner of Surrealism (since he described by the word "supernaturalism" a state so akin to Surrealism that André Breton has said that by it he "grasped the spirit marvelously"), Gérard de Nerval declared throughout the entire body of his work that the world of the imagination has a reality quite as great as that of the waking world. For him, the dream was a means of exploring his own nature, and in that way he gained access to supreme knowledge. Yet he could not discover its magic without first plumbing the depths of hell.

This investigation of another reality, by bringing it into

the light of day and analyzing it without inhibition, is the way of Surrealism, because Surrealism also "aspires to the total recovery of our physical powers by means amounting to a dizzy descent into ourselves, a systematic illumination of the hidden places, and the progressive occlusion of the other places."

The mind, left to its own resources, moves in a phantasmagorical world, where beings and objects take on unforeseen aspects and display themselves in dreamlike colors. As Bergson has pointed out, the dream state is implacably opposed to practical reality, in which, influenced by immediate concerns, we isolate only those facts that are immediately useful. If we can detach ourselves, closing our eyes, then we are carried into a galaxy of images and suppressed memories that sweep us beyond all the confines of logic and reason. For Freud, this world is the representation of our unconscious desires and repressed inclinations, and man, by deciphering its symbols, will attain an integrated understanding of himself. We voluntarily consign this richness to the shadows so that we can act practically, so that we can succeed in life, and in doing so we mutilate our very existence. Moreover, André Breton deplores that "these acts of reparation" occurring in sleep are not better rewarded "than by the disfavor that makes almost every man a *guilty* sleeper."

If the life of dreams asserts itself as being at least as important as waking life, why should we not keep tally of the disclosures it can bring us? "Can my last night's dream perhaps follow on from that of the night before, and will it not be continued the following night with commendable precision?" Memory recalls to us only fragments of dreams, not their totalities; our waking life is no more than a focal agent under that other life's sway. Why is one being attracted by another? "Isn't the thing he likes about a certain woman *exactly* related to something in his dream, linked by attributes his waking self has lost?" As Salvador Dali writes in *La Femme Visible*, "By day we unconsciously search for the lost images of our dreams, and that is why, when we find such an image, we believe we are already familiar with it, and say that to see it is to dream." Cannot the dream—symbol of the repressed world and Surreality's domain—be employed, asks André Breton, to solve "life's fundamental problems"?

In dreams everything seems easy, everything seems natural, "the tormenting question of possibility does not arise." The mind, passive before the most extraordinary happenings, only deems them contradictory upon waking, when, subjected to our strict and limited logic, "the slightest dream is more perfect than the slightest poem, since by definition it is perfectly satisfying to the dreamer."

It may be objected that what we call real, although no more than an infinitely small part of the mystery in which we are involved, ought not to be rejected out of hand in its familiar aspect, since the dream itself is no more than another expression of the waking state. Yet ought we not rather to say with Pascal, "Who knows if this other half of life in which we think we are awake is not merely a somewhat different sort of sleep, from which we wake when we think we go to sleep?" This argument—also dear to the skeptics—which refuses all reality to the world we live in, can have value, according to André Breton, only "if the experience of believing ourselves awake when we sleep is balanced by the experience of believing ourselves asleep when we are awake"—and this latter condition is rather exceptional. On the contrary, comparisons of "sleep's presentations"—dreams—with those of wakefulness show that they share existence and are also real.

The evoking of dreams in other beings also allows "the fathoming of the complete individual nature in a total way that includes past, present, and future." Dreaming is a means to knowledge just as much as thinking, and it should be analyzed under the same heading. Dreaming is no longer just a mental indulgence, but one of the most significant activities, and in this sense Surrealism approaches Hindu philosophy. Indeed, in the Vedanta, the three states of wakefulness, the dream, and deep sleep are analyzed separately, and are thought of as diverse aspects of manifestation.

Western philosophy, in systematically neglecting those phenomena that evade reason, limits by just so much our knowledge of man and the universe. Thus Surrealism has had the originality to reinstate the dream, and to attribute to it psychological and metaphysical importance as great as, if not greater than, that of the waking state.

Madness

Surrealism, "the crossroads of sleep's enchantments, and those of alcohol . . . is also a breaker of chains." The incoherence and weirdness of dreams naturally cause us to reflect upon the disordered revelations of the insane, whose universe offers such possibilities for our better self-understanding. Those sufferers who are divorced from external reality "in being longer acquainted than us with the internal reality," according to Freud, "are able to reveal to us some things that, but for them, would remain impenetrable."

Indeed, in the world of the deranged imagination reigns as mistress. Their minds move buoyantly through the midst of contradictions and incoherences such as never occur to the man in the street. They are unadapted to everyday life, but for them their universe has as much certainty as ours. The study of their vagaries appreciably enlarges our field of knowledge, and carries us away from a practical and limited reality. Thus, in *Le Vampire,* a Surrealist novel dealing with hallucinations, we glimpse how the subjective life, developed to its maximum, enables manifestations of the unconscious to be observed at liberty, so to speak. Thanks to their magnification by a deranged mind, these normal phenomena can be examined as under a microscope.

These beings, who reject society because they are unable to adapt themselves, live in the world of dreams and fantasies, and give us fresh views of this territory where all is permitted.

Of the numerous mental disorders, one of them, paranoia, by offering a synthesis of the real and the imaginary, points toward the goal Surrealism seeks. The patient, afflicted by delusions of grandeur, or by persecution mania, is not content to take refuge in his interior world, but instead incorporates the attributes of the external world in his delusions. His impressions of the outside world serve only to illustrate his mental fantasies. Although he lives in the same universe as a normal man, experiencing the same sensations and sharing the same unfolding of events, he reacts in a totally different way, since, in his view, each event serves only to confirm his subjective necessities. If he believes himself to be a prince of the blood royal, he constructs family trees that will establish his relationship to such-and-such of the family's surviving contemporaries. He construes international events either as gestures of homage to his authority, or as attacks upon his dignity, and he believes that his actions or his words are the cause of this or that political occurrence. Such a delusion is perfectly coherent, and if we put ourselves in the place of the paranoiac, assuming the same point of departure, we find that his whole concept of the world can be deduced from it very logically. Besides, writes Salvador Dali, "all doctors agree in recognizing the inconceivable subtlety frequently encountered in paranoiacs, and the speed with which their minds work to provide facts and reasons of such niceness that they escape normal people entirely, yet lead to conclusions that are often impossible to refute . . . and which in any case, defy all analysis."

As the paranoiac sees it, the world is a theatre in which he is the principal actor. Nothing takes place in it in an objective manner, and, as in the world of primitive peoples, everything in it is infused with occult intentions that must be interpreted. This attitude is not so far from that of the normal man; and from the lunatic to the scientist, whose pretensions to vigorous objectivity have been denounced as illusory, passing en route the prejudiced individual who colors the world in terms of his own loves and hates, there is certainly more of a hierarchy than a rigid opposition, a hierarchy "that will then consist of noble orders, and amusement will be obtained by appointing to those orders men who have themselves an account to settle with human reason, that very reason which daily denies us the right to express ourselves by means that are, for us, instinctive." Moreover, all we learn about this world of illusion and paradox makes the psychiatrist's classifications seem extremely arbitary.

L'Immaculée Conception, the book in which André Breton and Paul Eluard successfully reclassify certain of the affective disorders, such as mental debility, acute dementia, general paralysis of the insane, obsessional delusions, and dementia praecox, demonstrates the malleability of the human mind, and shows that it is able to submit to insane ideas at will "without thereby incurring a prolonged disturbance, and without in any way damaging its faculty of balance." One such exercise at the outset brought to the authors a consciousness of "resources that until then were quite unsuspected" and, more than that, was a first step toward "the very highest state of freedom," since it allowed a total release from the constraints of an assumed good sense. The extent of the territory thus revealed is illustrated especially in the chapter entitled "Meditations," wherein the riches of the internal world are contrasted with all the shabbiness of our usual surroundings. "On the road that rebounds as obstinately as if tied to the feet of him that sets out along it today, just as he will set out tomorrow, and with no more guidance than heedlessness can afford, a thousand footsteps every day embrace the footsteps of the waking state. We have been there before, and we shall need no pressing to come again. Everyone has passed that way as he goes from happiness to misery. It is a tiny refuge lit by an immense gas jet. We put one foot in front of the other, and we have gone."

We can do no other than desire this enlargement of the field of human psychology, and "the profound detachment that the insane evince in regard to criticism directed at them leaves us to suppose that they draw great consolation from their imaginations, and that they savor their delirium sufficiently for it not to matter that it has not a general validity. In fact, hallucinations and illusions are a source of more than negligible delight. In them, the best regulated sensuality finds its place." In a letter to André Breton, Ernest de Gengenbach gives his reply to the doctor who implored him to renounce the dangers of automatic writing: "I prefer my agonizing and desperate spiritual measures to the logical and rational measures of intelligence."

Indeed, if we allow ourselves to be intoxicated by these adventures beyond the limits of reason, we risk being "devoured by the monster." It is because the Surrealists know how to resist what Jung calls "the temptation of morbid elation" that they can go so far as to risk reconstructing certain states of delirium. By keeping some contact with the external world they succeed in giving themselves up to these "mental gymnastics," even to the point of simulating madness, yet always remaining capable of returning to a normal state in due course. Just as it is humor that induces awareness of the ridiculous when applied to identifiable realities, so it is humor that is the guardian of spiritual integrity, and, in fact, part and parcel of all Surrealist manifestations.

Therefore, one of the objectives of Surrealism can be said to be "the creation of a mental state that no longer has anything to wish for from derangement." Necessarily, "the thought succumbs *in the end* to the thinkable," which is to say that the mind detaches itself from all prejudice and convention to let psychic automatism speak for it as a means of revelation. André Breton and Paul Eluard do not go so far as to pretend "that experiments in the simulation of mental disorders will advantageously take the place of the ballad, the sonnet, the epic, the poem without beginning or end, and other decaying forms."

The endeavor of these poets, then, has had the originality to isolate, in an experimental way, those workings of the mind that are purely automatic, and to evoke the untrammeled play of thought freed from all subjection to practical necessities. "And there," exclaims Maurice Nadeau, "Surrealism shows itself to be truly creative and brilliantly inventive. No risk of the movement staying buried in the pages of *L'Immaculée Conception,* now that he whose eyes have been opened will want nothing more than to prove his powers to the limits of his being."

Surrealist Objects

Mental derangement, by throwing back the frontiers of human knowledge, contributes to the discrediting of reality. The paranoiac, far from submitting passively to the visions of his imagination, uses them to interpret the objects of the external world by abstracting them from their normal purposes. His attitude resembles that of the humorist who, by attributing a grotesque character to objects, dismembers reality and, in doing so, propels the spirit into the realm of the Surreal. There is, however, this difference between them: one identifies himself with his visions, whereas the other, after his expeditions into the special zone, resumes his normal behavior.

It is precisely the paranoiac's privilege to demonstrate by what process illusions tend to become objective, to unite with reality, and that is what has led Salvador Dali to endow "Surrealism with an instrument of the first importance, a sort of *paranoiac-critical* method, which has shown itself to be fully capable of being applied indifferently to painting, to poetry, to cinema, to the making of typically Surrealist objects, to fashion, to sculpture, to art history, and even, on occasion, to every kind of exposition." According to him, the critical method that takes into consideration only "the exclusively passive and receptive role in regard to the Surrealist subject ought to be replaced by an active method capable of realizing materially a world delirious with concrete irrationality." Where essentially undeveloped and chimerical images cannot satisfy "our desires and our principles of verification," new ones must be cultivated "objectively, and on the plane of truth, as proved by Eluard and Breton's experiments in simulation," and also by the construction of Surrealist objects.

For instance, Salvador Dali proposed that "some enormous motorcars, three times larger than natural, should be reproduced (with a minutia of detail exceeding that of the most precise metal castings) in plaster or onyx, so that, wrapped in women's underlinen, they could be enclosed in sepulchers the sites of which will be marked only by a tiny clock made of straw." These bizarre vehicles illustrate his definition of the Surrealist object: "an object that lends itself to the minimum of mechanical functioning, and that is based upon fantasies and images capable of being induced by the substantiation of unconscious actions."

It was a dream that inspired André Breton to the construction of these objects, which are repressed desires taking form as concrete facts. Dreaming that he was in St. Malo, amid the stalls of a street market, he came upon "a rather curious book. Its spine was formed by a gnome carved in wood, and the gnome's white beard, somewhat Assyrian in style, reached all the way to his feet. The statuette's thickness was normal, yet it in no way hindered the turning of the book's pages, which were made of heavy, black wool." Breton was eager to buy it and, on awakening, was so disappointed by not having it that he decided to construct those objects "that only come our way in dreams, and that can be defended less on the grounds of usefulness than on those of charm; and that, by throwing the greatest discredit on 'reasonable' people and objects, perhaps will contribute to the downfall of those representational trophies that are so detestable."

It was such Surrealist objects, perhaps even more than the poems and paintings, that disconcerted the public. They contributed to the dreamlike and mysterious atmosphere that greeted visitors to the Surrealist exhibition of 1938. Unfortunately, as Rolland de Reneville deplored, "the ravishing manikins disposed in the lobby of the exhibition that represented the spirit of falling asleep, and the mission of which was to introduce the dreamer gradually to the hypnagogic realm," were seen by many of the visitors "merely as childish puppets."

The Exquisite Corpse

Any means whatever are good if they lead to the breaking up of our regimentation so that we can take cognizance of our hidden wealth. The point is simply to achieve emptiness in order to let the unconscious express itself spontaneously. If each of us, on his own account, tries to encompass this experience, we can presently put to work the resources of a group to induce it by a procedure analogous to that of the game of Pass It On. Several people get together and, in turn, pass each other a sheet of paper on which a word is written, or an outline traced; they end up with a sequence of improbable phrases, or a drawing that defies all reality. "The example that has become classic, and the first element of which, obtained in this way, has given its name to the game, is: 'The exquisite corpse—will drink —the new wine.' "

This procedure, so apt for the forming of pure and striking Surrealist images, gives rise to such phrases as "the feathered steam seduces the padlocked bird" and "the oyster from Senegal will eat the tricolored bread," and drawings such as a crab-headed man. Paul Eluard tells us of "evenings passed in creating, with affection, a whole race of 'exquisite corpses.' We competed to see who could get the most charm, the most unity, and the most audacity into this poetry composed collectively. No more worries, and no more thought of unhappiness, boredom, or the daily round. We played with the images, and there were no losers. . . . If one of us asked a question, anxiety or pleasure were involved solely in the answer given. Each player wrote his question without disclosing it, posing it, as it were, to himself, and someone replied confidently in order to learn the question."

If the game takes place between two questioners, the dialogue might go like this:

S.—What is the moon?
B.—It is a marvelous glacier.
N.—What is spring?
S.—A lamp fueled by glowworms.
A. A.—Has Surrealism invariably the same importance in the organization of our life as in its disorganization?
A. B.—It is the mud into whose composition hardly any flowers are introduced.

IN THIS UNIVERSE of analogies every object is One Within Another, according to the title of a game invented by the Surrealists a score of years later.

Thus, The Exquisite Corpse encourages man to release himself from the world of dismal reality, so that he can penetrate the world of the disjointed and the strange. Those who surrender to the game can disentangle themselves from their personalities, letting automatism come to the fore.

Automatic Writing

These various Surrealist techniques aim only at the rejection of civilization's encumbrances, so that man may be revealed as he is in himself, in his primitive state, and so that in the end he may recover all his psychological power and become truly free.

By relaxing all efforts at control in states such as the dream and madness, the unconscious reveals itself spontaneously; and automatic writing can transcribe its messages. André Breton made this discovery when in a state halfway between dreaming and waking. Some phrases took form in his mind and struck him "as being poetic elements of the first order." The words were as if "pronounced in a stage whisper," and they brought a feeling of exceptional certainty to his mind. In the *Premier Manifeste du Surréalisme,* he tells how, one night just as he was falling asleep, he was roused to attention by a bizarre phrase, clearly articulated, and quite unrelated to the activities of the day, "a phrase that seemed to me peremptorily insistent, a phrase—dare I say it?—*that tapped on the window.*" This was accompanied by a visual representation that, on his awakening, gave him an extremely strong impression of something never seen. These personal experiences suggested to him that he might put himself voluntarily into this receptive state, while noting immediately the spontaneous unfolding of his impressions. "Wholly preoccupied by Freud," he resolved to obtain from himself, as mental patients do from themselves, "a flowing monologue as rapid as possible, upon which the subject's critical faculties were to pass no judgment, which was not to be inhibited by any reticence, and which would be as nearly as possible the *spoken thought.*"

In order to plunge himself into this state, he had naturally to isolate himself from the importunities of the outside world. Together with Philippe Soupault, Breton trained himself to let his unconscious speak, and under its dictation the two wrote *Les Champs Magnétiques*, which is only "the first application of this discovery; each chapter has no reason to end other than the ending of the day upon which it was undertaken and, from one chapter to the next, only the variation of tempo characterizes results that, otherwise, differ little." This book is rich in brilliant, unexpected, and humorous comparisons. To quote a few: "Well-loved books build our prison, but from ourselves we can no longer escape by means of all those ardent scents that lull us to sleep. . . . Everyone can pass along that bleeding corridor where our sins hang from hooks, a charming picture, in which, however, the gray predominates."

These images impose themselves on the thought in a quite specific way: "To you who write, each element seems as strange as another, and naturally you challenge yourself concerning it." As a practitioner of Surrealism who has

undertaken the experience comments, unknown sensations
gradually invade the mind:

> A. It produces astonishing plays on words, appropriate
> to Surrealism, and abstracted from a turmoil of sounds.
> . . . The thought passes above the words like a storm.
> B. In another of these states . . . the mind is trans-
> fixed in a dramatic atmosphere.
> . . . It is an apocalypse that escapes from itself.
> C. The mind follows an irregular course . . .
> . . . During automatic writing the consciousness
> should be quite blank—this is the most desirable state. . . .
> The thought's pure transition should not be accompanied by
> any sensation inimical to its development.
> In this way the mind will supply the dictation quite
> dispassionately and in its own terms.

The external world slips away to such a degree that any
interruption to the writing is like an abrupt awakening:
"Your eyes no longer take in the surrounding objects, your
legs shake under you. . . ."

This technique had already been employed in the
eighteenth century, an age rich in extravagantly romantic
novels, in which the fantastic and the real incessantly
mingle. On this subject, André Breton quotes one of Horace
Walpole's letters to William Cole disclosing the genesis of
one of his works, *The Castle of Otranto*. The book was inspired by a dream, and Walpole composed it in a purely
spontaneous way while in a sort of transcendent state.

Joachim von Arnim was one of the first to use automatic writing as a means of freeing himself from the constraints of premeditated thought. However, André Breton considers that automatic writing ought to be accessible to everyone, and without making use of the techniques of hypnosis. It seems to him to achieve what Schrenck Notzing hoped to find in hypnosis: the knowledge "of a reliable means of helping the flights of the mental faculties, and especially artistic talent, by concentrating the unconscious on the task in hand, and by releasing the individual from the inhibitions that restrain him and disturb him, sometimes to the point of absolutely frustrating the exercise of his latent gifts." The mind should be completely passive and, by suppressing all conscious talent, it should transcribe only this "magic dictation." It should let the words follow one another without making any attempt to understand them.

The forms of the Surrealist language best adapt themselves to duologues, because the meeting of two minds gives rise to images even more unexpected than in monologues, provided that each speaker "simply pursues his own soliloquy without seeking to draw any particular dialectical pleasure from it, and without imposing it in the slightest degree upon his colleague's territory." Each man speaks for himself, and that is how the chapter "Barriers" originated in the *Champs Magnétiques*.

These various plunges into the unconscious are expressed by images of great poetic beauty—poetry being better adapted than painting for suggesting the mysterious depths, by reason of its lesser involvement with matter and greater quickness at translating the untrammeled mind's thought-stream. André Breton "maintains that verbal inspirations are infinitely richer in visual sense, and make an infinitely stronger impression upon the eye, than what are properly called visual images," and goes as far as to protest against "the pretended visionary power of the poet." He even contends that "Lautréamont and Rimbaud have not seen, have not enjoyed a priori what they describe, which is the equivalent of saying that they have not described it; lurking in the darkened wings of existence, they hear the players' lines but indistinctly, and put down what they hear. . . . The *Illuminations* is the result."

Soundings taken in the subliminal self have significance only if they enrich the concept of man, his knowledge of himself and of the world, of which he is no more than a fragment. Surrealism demands that

those who, in the Freudian sense, have "the precious gift" of which we speak should apply themselves to study the mechanism of inspiration by the light of day. Once they cease to think of inspiration as something sacred, and with all the confidence they have in its extraordinary qualities, they must dream only of throwing off its bonds and—something that was hitherto inconceivable—making it submit. . . . We readily discover in this prize the total possession of our minds. . . . We discover the nature of the short circuit it induces between a given concept and its interpreter. . . . In poetry and in painting Surrealism has achieved the impossible in multiplying these short circuits. It does not claim, and it never will, to reproduce artificially that imaginary moment when man, at the mercy of a particular emotion, is suddenly gripped by something "stronger than him," which hurls him involuntarily into the ineffable. Awakened and lucid, it is with terror that he will emerge from that false step. The whole of it is that he will still not be free, that he will continue to speak for as long as the mysterious tintinnabulation goes on, and indeed, it is there that he ceases to be part of what we are part of.

These products of psychic activity, that is to say, automatic writing and the accounts of dreams, should be engendered in conditions as free as possible from all idea of responsibility, such as are always ready to act as fetters, and as independent as possible of everything that does not pertain to the *passive life of the intelligence*. These products present certain advantages in that they alone supply some elements of appreciation in the grand style to a contemporary criticism that shows itself to be strangely at sixes and sevens, by encouraging a general reclassification of lyrical values, and by offering a key that, having the power to open indefinitely this box with many bottoms called "man," dissuades him from turning away (as he might, from instincts of plain conservation) when he stumbles into the shadow of those doors that are closed from outside on reality's "beyond," the source of genius and love.

Thus the road opened by revolt and by destruction ends in a universe of enchantment where all raptures are permitted, and where the language is precisely this automatic writing. From these brilliant encounters of images flashes a surprising beauty that only artists can express. Are not the poets "the superiors of us, the ordinary men, since they quench their thirst at springs that have not yet been provided for us by science"?

2 / Art and Surreality

Poetry

Great courage is needed in him who ventures upon the quicksands of the unconscious "for the sole sake of casting a handful of foam-flecked green seaweed here and there upon the beach." Some poets can find this courage because the beauty of the images disclosed makes them oblivious to the obstacles the world places in the way of their dreams. As René Crevel sees it, "Poetry throws bridges from one sense to another, from the object to the image, from the image to the idea, and from the idea to the precise fact. Poetry is a road through the particles of a world that has been isolated by mundane expediencies, a road that leads toward exciting encounters, as testified by the paintings and collages of Dali, Ernst, and Tanguy. It is the road to freedom."

Traditional education either underestimates or conspires to repress the poet's spontaneous transports, refusing to see in them the component factors of a true flowering, and it is the liberation of these transports from automatic patterns that must be achieved in a desperate effort to free poetry from all its shackles and to release it from vassalage to morals and logic. For the artist who discerns the marvelous beyond the real, the whole world will become clothed in poetry: advertisements, placards, and newspaper clippings thrown together at random make poems, since whatever tears an object from its normal purpose propels it into the Surreal, just as the association of scraps of differentiated images or sentences routs the spirit of reality, and projects it into another universe. Says Tristan Tzara, "You can be a poet without ever writing a single verse . . . poetry exists in the street, in a business exhibition, or anywhere at all."

The whole of life becomes a pretext for poetry. "An everyday fact can be the starting point: for the poet a falling handkerchief can be the lever with which he raises a whole universe." Almost any action, however seemingly insignificant, can be the source of a revelation to anyone with the gift of effacing himself until he is no more than the instrument of a voice expressing itself through his being. Every man is a poet who ignores himself, and he has only to turn from his limited horizon for enchantments far surpassing it to open up for him.

By contrast, the work of a Paul Valéry, in which the literary problems take "the shape of abstractions, of theoretical limits, and of the impure," serves only to invoke the revolt of those who hold in contempt all in literature that is calculated. "*Anthinea,* the glorification of solid things, and, on the other hand, the *Poisson Soluble,* are two opposed symbols: a neo-classicism, and a neo-romanticism," observes Albert Thibaudet. And the Surrealists can only be indignant at this statement of Valéry's: "In all conscience, I would infinitely rather write something feeble than bring forth, with the help of a trance, a masterpiece ranking among the most beautiful." So, about 1921, as Jean Paulhan recalls, the Surrealists parted from this poet in order to plunge into the labyrinth of the instinctive and of the vital. "Sooner madness than artifice and calculation," they wrote.

In investigating authentic life, these new Romantics believed that retouching could only disfigure this Surreality so difficult to envisage. As Paul Eluard says:

> Hallucination, frankness, fury, memory, this lunatic Proteus, these ancient histories, the table and the inkstand, the unknown passages, the turning night, the sudden recollections, prophecies inspired by passion, the conflagration of ideas, feelings and things, the blind nakedness, the systematic ventures toward useless ends growing to supreme utility, the derangement of logic into absurdity, the practice of the

absurd until it becomes indomitable reason—it is these and not the more or less skillful, more or less happy, combination of consonants, syllables, and words, that contribute to a poem's harmony. It must voice a musical thought, making drums, violins, rhythms, and rhymes fashion a terrible concert for the ears of asses.

According to this conception, art is a liberation of the spirit from its limits that at last makes possible the flight of pure inspiration.

Thus, for the Surrealists, the important thing is to leave the confines of reality while at the same time going beyond the illusory theories of art for art's sake. For André Breton, "Poetry ought to lead somewhere," and his disciples expect from their unconscious the revelation of Surreality's mysteries.

The Surrealist is properly an "inspired being," because he only prides himself on that for which he is least responsible. Thus, relates André Breton, "Each morning, at the moment of wakening, Saint-Pol-Roux, not long ago, used to put a notice on the door of his manor at Camaret, on which could be read 'The poet labors.'" What disdain of the poetic "exercise," dear to Paul Valéry, has this concept, according to which "the principle of total inspiration is ruined by the least erasure. . . . Stupidity effaces what the ear has skillfully *created*. . . . What pride in writing, without knowing either language or verb . . . neither to conceive the *structure* of the work's duration, nor the conditions of its ending; nothing at all of the *why,* and nothing at all of the *how!*" For the Surrealists "perfection is *idleness.*"

Thus, voluntary effort must be banished, since discrimination will affect the purity of inspiration by risking the tarnishing of the views that one seeks to coax from the unknown.

> Indeed, it is remarkable that from Baudelaire and Poe as far as Mallarmé, a powerful tendency—the author of *Charmes* was affected by it, and has clearly asserted its effects—has persuaded certain writers only to preoccupy themselves with tenacity and perfect *attention,* while the Surrealist poets, heirs of Rimbaud and Lautréamont, claim on the other hand that the whole secret of creativeness rests essentially in the dream state, which rightly represents the point at which the human mind can normally attain the greatest degree of *indifference.*

As Louis Aragon has put it, inspiration is "the ability to dispose the human mind and heart to the Surreal in the most authentic way." At the other extreme, the disciples of Mallarmé and Valéry stretch their spiritual energies to the fullest extent in attempting to seize to themselves the divine power of the Creator.

To illustrate these divergent attitudes toward the mystery of the cosmos, Rolland de Reneville suggests that the reader imagine for an instant that his mind is "an imaginary circle" in the middle of which dwells "an image of his consciousness whilst the areas lying between the central point and the perimeter of the circle represent the pure realm of his unconscious." The Surrealists endeavor to suppress this center of consciousness, aiming to identify themselves with the Infinite, since, for them, as for Rimbaud, "the first study of the man who wishes to be a poet is a complete knowledge of himself; . . . he must make of himself an immense soul. . . ." By abandoning themselves to their inspiration, the Surrealists endeavor to attain to the unity of the universe, to become the messengers of the gods, as were the oracles of antiquity. "If, with Louis Aragon, we consider that consciousness obtains no part of its elements from anywhere except within the unconscious, we are obliged to acknowledge that consciousness is contained within the unconscious."

There is, then, a conflict between this concept and that of the poets, who strive to give such an importance to the circle's central point "that this nucleus ends up by gathering in the frontiers of the unconscious until, by gradually absorbing them into its own illuminating authority, it makes them vanish. This progressive enlargement of the center of consciousness will be the result of an implacable and voracious *attention*, the object of which will have little significance, since it will have no other end than its own intensity. Soon this immense illumination will have extended itself to the spirit's entirety." And, for Paul Valéry, in *Variétés*, "the true condition of the true poet is that which pertains most distinctly to the dream state."

The single end of these two methods always remains the absolute, whence the original, though ephemeral, sympathy that existed between Paul Valéry and André Breton. The ambivalence of their positions had been precisely anticipated in this phrase of Baudelaire's: "From the convergence of myself and from the dispersion of myself—there lies the whole of it." And, according to inclination, some poets strive to sculpt their poems in the hope that a new reality will spring up from the meticulous combinations of words, and others plunge into the bowels of the universe to arrive at the source of the mystery.

IT was only after this fishing in troubled waters that the Surrealists, wishing to understand the revelations of their art, formulated their metaphysical and psychological tenets. In fact, André Breton says that poetry ought to suggest "a specific solution to the problem of life." It is only a means of access to certain vast lands that "art—constrained for centuries from deviating from the well-trodden paths of ego and superego—must show itself eager to explore."

The poet will be able to inspire himself with Gothic novels, those fairy tales for adults that use as springboards "fear, the appeal of the unusual, hazards, and the taste for luxury." The expression of these repressed instincts will perhaps rescue the poet from his incurable disquiet. As Georges Hugnet has pointed out, Surrealism has enabled poetry to take an immense step. "From literature and—may I say it?—from paper, poetry has slipped into the very heart of life. It is no longer an art, a spiritual state, but life and the spirit itself. It is a way of feeling and of experiencing, a way of using sight and double-sight, a method of knowledge."

Thus, for André Breton and Paul Eluard poetry can be defined as "the endeavor to represent, or restore, in *articulated language tending to express itself obscurely, those things* or *that thing* in which there is the appearance of life or something of life's supposed purpose, and this by means of cries, tears, and endearments . . . or by means of objects. That thing has the nature of that energy which refuses to respond to what exists."

The poet's personality vanishes beneath this overflowing torrent, and he becomes the echo of cosmic harmonies, the echo of the universe's mysterious resonance. The Surrealists, freed from Valéry's influence, found that to some degree they had amassed a poetry endowed with immense dynamism that surges from the very bowels of existence, in a river of liberating mud. "For some years," wrote André Breton, "I have counted on the torrential supply of automatic writing for the ultimate cleansing of the literary stables. In this respect, the desire to throw wide the floodgates will remain, without any doubt, the generative concept of Surrealism."

The insurgents, revolting against the world and against God, could at the outset only sink themselves into the depths of sensuality and sin. In this return to primitive chaos, where all is confusion, the poets had, by virtue of their exceptional sensitivity, the unique privilege of understanding, at long intervals, true objectivity. The genuine artist does not express a particular and individual emotion, but penetrates to the deep roots of human nature. The Surrealists, at the start of their researches, did not probe their inner natures in order to combat their desires and instincts, but on the contrary, gave them free run. "A poem should be a disaster of the intellect." They penetrated not at all into a transcendent world, but into the realm of the instincts, and that is why their works are peopled by monsters, since "the flora and fauna of Surrealism are unavowable." From *La Liberté ou L'Amour* comes the impression "that our restricted individuality communicates with an infinite that is paradisaical and obscene." According to Gabriel Bounoure, this book by Robert Desnos expresses "the pure and simple fact of living, desire in its primordial frenzy, and the sexually marvelous . . . with a gloomy grandeur that places reality beneath the sway of the fantastic, this being what the Surrealist experience consists of."

In this way, although not belonging to the Surrealist movement, Pierre-Jean Jouve, in a work such as *Sueur de Sang*, "attains the Surreal by way of the Under-Real. . . . He urges himself to know the worst of himself, those monsters that are in us, sleeping or waking, and that are not entirely of us, because it is first from these standpoints that the universe must be regarded, *at the peril of our life and of our love.*" His stories, contrasting the civilized world with original chaos, are the *Histoires Sanglantes* (Bleeding

Stories) of the conflict "between a spirit's present entity and its hidden forces."

Thus, description of the lowest of human corruptions draws the attention to a region generally left in the shadow. Yet this "cleansing with ordure," indispensable to him who wants to free himself from his desires, is only the point of departure toward a higher reality.

Indeed, it is not because the poet lets himself be guided by his unconscious that his work will have direction. "The man holding the pen does not anticipate what he is about to write, and he ignores both what he writes and what he finds written when he comes to read it," says Louis Aragon. "A life of which he has not the secret controls his hand, and, since he feels himself unconcerned, it seems to him that he writes just anything. But it would certainly be a mistake to conclude that what is written there is really unimportant. What is unimportant is what you write when you compose an ordinary letter, for instance, because then you are at the mercy of your own arbitrary attitudes. Surrealism, however, is a stern master—inevitably stern. The sense is formed outside your consciousness. The groups of words end by meaning something truly significant, instead of, as in the other instance, expressing themselves only fragmentarily."

No manifestation of the spirit is to be despised, and: "In the Surrealist experience, everything takes place as if it were the curve of a graph of whose terms we know nothing. By what possible means can you discuss this curve's variations? Its peaks, its dips, and its interruptions have value because they express the unknown. It is in quest of this unknown that those who follow the present experiment have launched themselves." Louis Aragon then eliminates those mediocre souls who see in these experiences only a "dodge" where they should see inspiration. "Thus, the gist of a Surrealist text is important in the highest degree—it is what gives it its precious character of a revelation."

IT IS NOT only its profound content that provides the value of such poetry, but also its form. Differing from the classic writer who describes reality as it is presented to us all, the Surrealist writer transmits the vibrations of the interior world, and in consequence, his expressions will be stamped with their mystery. As Rimbaud has written, if what the poet "reports from the depths of his being has form, he reproduces form. If it is formless, he ignores form." It is difficult to translate the universe of the dream by means of normal language, so it is often necessary to invest it with an unexpected import. Habit hides from us the power of the most hackneyed words to surprise, but to ears that have the gift of staying young they convey freshness and poetry. Also, as Pierre-Jean Jouve points out apropos of his work *Vagadu,* the reader of Surrealist works "needs an altogether special spiritual attitude. Instead of aiming to understand clearly at first try, he should respond to the varied, but insistent, images, as they pass before his eyes." If he puts the accumulations of an artificial culture from his mind, he will enable it to be flooded by the torrents of his interior life.

As with automatic writing, the poem permits a man to glimpse a new world, and to balance its elements with those of the rational world. "Reduced, then, to equality, they intermingle and, compounding, form poetic unity." Thus, in this accord between content and form, genuine Surrealist poems can also measure up to the Kantian criterion of beauty. Besides, Surrealism has its *Traité du Style* (Treatise on Style) and, according to its author, Louis Aragon, "There is a striking method by which we seek to discriminate between Surrealist texts—by their force and by their novelty. And, as with dreams, they have to be well written." Moreover, a Belgian critic, Louis Carette, asserts that "it is form and style that will bear *Nadja* and *Le Paysan de Paris* down the rivers of posterity."

BERGSON also maintained that discursive language was powerless to render the imponderable in a way that the intuition could grasp. This can only be attempted by means of concrete images that suggest it to the reader. Necessarily, if we aim at spiritual ascesis, we must address ourselves to the imagination and the senses, rather than to the intelligence.

Always it is spontaneity that, driving the Surrealist's

pen, produces that strange phantasmagoria which overthrows our artistic concepts. Moreover, André Breton is against all aesthetic or moral attempts "to impose a formal beauty upon a work by means of conscious improvement that will necessarily appertain to the man who carries it out." Beauty springs "from the image as it takes form in automatic writing," and it must be considered convulsive in nature. Lautréamont's "as beautiful as" constitutes the manifesto of this new poetry.

We must distinguish carefully, with Jacques Rivière, between images used by men of letters to "reinforce an idea" or "to sharpen the senses in the same way as the intelligence," and the pure image as used by the Surrealists, who express it as "a group of words corresponding matchlessly to the thing seen, with nothing to betray the relationship between the words and the vision and with nothing that serves to integrate the image with any intellectual system. The whole of post-Dadaist poetry is an immense heap of these images, in which, if we use intuition as a magnifying glass, we can see the movements of stars and angels across immeasurable distances."

The most forceful images are also the most arbitrary, the most contradictory, and the most difficult to express. They disconcert both reason and the senses, and make everything participate in everything else. A dreamlike atmosphere, and intense poetry, are engendered by the works that express this enchanted universe. Even their titles are evocative, such as *Le Poisson Soluble* (The

Soluble Fish), which is an unexpected way of saying that "man is soluble in his thought." The mind, letting itself be swept along by this brilliant enchantment, will be "carried along by images that ravish it . . . it is the most beautiful of all nights, *the night of gleaming lightning,* and after it, the day is the night."

From *Revolver à Cheveux Blancs,* we extract some further images: "A pearl necklace for which no clasp can be found, and for which the whole of existence contains no thread—there is hopelessness. . . . In its broad outlines, despair has no importance. It is a gang of trees that make a forest, it is a gang of stars that make a missing day, it is a gang of missing days that make a life."

André Breton wants, then, "to climb once more to the sources of the poetic imagination . . . now an arrow indicates the direction of these countries, and the gaining of the true end no longer depends upon the traveler's endurance." Thought, left to itself, is so quickly invaded by a phantasmagoria of images that Louis Aragon has written, "We have lost the power to control them; we have become theirs, and they ride us."

The unexpected relationships between remote realities should owe nothing to conscious intention. André Breton denies that the images of Pierre Reverdy, such as "There is a song in the brook that trickles" or "The day has unfolded itself like a white cloth" or, yet again, "The world retreats into a sack," betray the slightest degree of premeditation. "Where we show ourselves infinitely sensitive is in the relationship, to some degree fortuitous, of two terms that spark off a particular light, *the light of the image.*" These elements are not united for the sake of the spark produced, but are the simultaneous products of the activity that André Breton calls Surrealist, in contrast to reason, which limits itself to establishing and appreciating the luminous phenomenon.

And just as a spark gains duration if it is projected through rarefied gas, the Surrealist atmosphere created by automatic writing especially lends itself to the production of the most beautiful images. It can even be said that the images displaying themselves in this heady way are the only banners of the spirit.

So, "By expressing the agony of its time, Surrealism has succeeded in giving a new face to beauty."

AN EXCURSION into this "forbidden zone" leads to a world invested with such great allure that the adventurer who ventures into it no longer thinks of retracing his steps. Surrealism, by its mysterious effects and particular pleasures, is a *new vice,* revealing paradises comparable to those proferred by hashish. Under its influence the whole of life seems to take refuge in a sort of mobile intoxication, which makes reason stagger and opens the door of the unknown. "I announce to the world"—exclaimed Louis Aragon, in *Le Paysan de Paris*—"this news of the first magnitude—a new vice has just been born, one more madness is granted to mankind, Surrealism, the son of frenzy and of shadow. Come in, come in, for here begin the realms of the instantaneous. The awakened sleepers of the Thousand and One Nights—the miraculously possessed and the epileptics —what have these that you modern hashish-takers should envy? Even without their instruments, you can run the gamut of their wonderful pleasures—some they have not even tasted themselves. For you are possessed of such visionary power over the world that neither reason nor any instinct to preservation is strong enough to prevent you from drinking deep of this vice. . . . The vice called Surrealism is the lawless and impassioned use of the image that amazes, or rather, the uncontrolled stimulation of the image for its own sake, and for the sake of what it entices into the field of representation in the way of metamorphoses and unforeseeable cataclysms; for each image with each shock forces you to revise the whole universe . . . magnificent spoliations: the principle of utility will become irrelevant to everyone who indulges this superlative vice."

In the sphere of the Surreal, we are far from the world of clear ideas and known facts. Yet it is true that the variety of the images, and their incoherence, exist only in regard to our normal classifications, oriented as they are toward the practical. The poet, on the other hand, with his acute sensitivity, grasps their profound analogies, the source from which they emanate and to which he desires to return. The image can even be defined as "the spirit's unity rediscovered in the multifariousness of matter." And Pierre

Gueguen considers it "a magic form of the principle of identity." At a time when, for so many contemporary poets, disorder is only the opposite of order, for others, aspiring to loftier summits, its diabolic aspect is the reflection of a superior rule. Their visions, in conflict and collision with each other, destroy themselves and thereby disencumber the spirit, leaving it purified and empty, so to speak. It is by the accumulation "of images of nothingness, such as snow or the night" that Paul Eluard, according to Rolland de Reneville, evokes "the presence of a unique entity" dwelling behind the various forms of love's manifestations, since it is by a dialectic of love that we ascend from the many faces of women to the ideal woman. "When extremely young"— writes Eluard, in *Donner à Voir*—"I opened my arms to purity. It was no more than a beating of wings in the sky of my eternity, no more than a beating of the heart, that lover's heart which beats in conquered breasts. No longer can I fall like that."

Yet this "discovery of the identity of the loved being with the absolute has its counterpart on the moral plane," in man's incurable isolation, which is the expression of his estrangement from transcendent unity. In fact, one of Paul Eluard's poems has for its title, *Univers-Solitude*. Its poetry "scintillates in an interstellar silence closed in the Surreal nakedness of pure existence, daughter of the concrete instant that flashes and dies in the dream."

Thus art, for the Surrealists, is a means of access to Surreality. Thus their works are not, strictly speaking, poetic, since, in addition, André Breton counsels us to "*practice* poetry" in order to attain this supreme revelation. "Literary pleasure or emotion is no longer but a particular instance of the still mysterious laws that govern the spirit's fundamental activities."

PREMEDITATED THOUGHT encroaches upon spontaneity in proportion to the degree to which society has developed. Among primitive peoples the dream still remains a means of knowledge, and poets are truly prophets. Later, a barrier arises between the subjective and objective worlds, and then, unfortunately, the dream no longer serves as "an instrument of diagnosis for all the neuroses and mental disorders."

It is also important to throw down the arbitrary separations that divide man, and in this respect Tristan Tzara considers that the poet has a genuine mission to fulfill, for is he not the champion of that disinterested activity which he strives to externalize and make predominate? The poet's symbols project "onto the external world, indirectly and in a higher form, facts corresponding to those that lie in a latent state beneath the external world's foundations. The relatively static is transformed into the relatively dynamic, and the inhibitory qualities of the dream are transformed into the exhibitory qualities of poetry." Poetry as "an activity of the spirit" ought to take the place of poetry as "means of expression," propaganda, and moralizing.

The true poet is, essentially, revolutionary, since he alone attempts, spurning all desire for security, to identify himself with the irrational forces that are the fundamentals of our true nature. Poetry transcends by far the words and images used in its expression, just as it transcends its social conditions. "The fact is, it embraces thought's purposes in all their complex totality. Indeed, even thought's functioning gravitates round poetry, whereas poetry raises thought, surpasses it, and denies it in its purpose."

Painting, Collage, and Cinema

Since, alone, dream images can suggest the intoxication of regained freedom, many artists have materialized their dreams, no longer by means of words, but by means of color. Indeed, painting is a "field of influence vaster than poetry," provided it "can be freed from the cares of exactly reproducing forms taken from the external world." Painting "should not have visual pleasure for its end," its aim being to make "our abstract knowledge take a step forward."

The Surrealists make the art critics despair by annihilating the concept of talent, and by asserting that Surrealist painting is a medium for artists in quest of true revelations, and prepared to subjugate themselves to inspiration. The painter's part being reduced to the minimum, "No conscious mental control goes into the making of a work that deserves to be qualified as absolutely Surrealist, since the active part of what has hitherto been called the *creator* is suddenly found to be reduced in the extreme, and just as the poet's role is to write to the dictation of his inner and unconscious thoughts (as they articulate themselves), so the painter's role, according to Max Ernst, is to encompass and project his inner vision." Moreover, Salvador Dali avows that there is nothing astonishing in the public's failure to understand his pictures, since he does not understand them himself. Since he seeks to reproduce the images of paranoiac delirium, for him they can only be "genuinely unknown" and of "hallucinatory character." "All explanation then arises a posteriori once the picture exists as an actuality." Thus, in one of them, we can see "six simultaneous images that are in no way representationally distorted—an athlete's torso, a lion's head, a general's head, a horse, the bust of a shepherdess, and a skull. Different spectators see different images in the picture," and each interprets it in his own way according to his temperament, just as different people hearing a symphony experience different emotions.

Furthermore, the various arts can be considered to be different means of interpreting the same intuition. Certain Surrealists, such as Arp and Dali, express themselves alike "in the poetic form or the plastic," and André Breton maintains "that there is no difference in the fundamental aspiration between a poem by Paul Eluard or Benjamin Peret and a canvas by Max Ernst, Miro, or Tanguy." So Salvador Dali, in *La Metamorphose de Narcisse,* adds to his poem a picture, a "diptych in which twin figures apparently represent comparable likenesses—in the first is Narcissus absorbed in his own reflection, and in the second, a stone hand holds an egg from which sprouts the famous flower. The poem and the painting are complementary," asserts André Lhote. For the first time, "A picture and a poem, both Surrealist, objectively admit of a coherent interpretation of an irrational subject."

Thus painting, like poetry, is the expression of man's second life. One of Chirico's canvases, which depicts "an enormous woman in marble lying on a wooden chest that has a railway for its base, the whole painted in housepainter's colors, cannot," according to Jacques Rivière, "have any significance of a strictly aesthetic order, but conveys to the soul an ambiguous emotion that comes of not knowing whether a world is created or a vision revealed." Chirico was a poet as well, and Paul Eluard looks upon the author of *Hebdomeros* as the painter of the world's "interior metaphysics." According to José Pierre, Kandinsky, from 1910 to 1919, also constructed "a world from which visions pluck themselves like so many images from the invisible." A work of art can only be truly immortal if it utterly leaves human limits behind, departing thereby from sound sense and logic.

THE SURREALISTS pushed to its extremes one concept of painting toward which a number of artists were already oriented. In spite of the Surrealists' contempt for Impressionism as such, they nevertheless carried on the movement engendered by that school, which sought only to hint at objects, the better to turn toward inner consciousness.

They likewise submitted to the influence of Cezanne, "Rimbaud's spiritual brother" and—according to André Lhote—"the father of the pictorial Surrealism that will reign tomorrow." Yet, for the Surrealists, it was Cubism that was the real revelation, with its disintegration of solid forms by material means, and its freeing of itself from practical necessities, thus helping to deliver man from routine.

Above all, it was to Picasso that André Breton extended his admiration, because he had been the first to impose on art a certain direction "outside the law," in that he sought to exile objects, as it were, by tearing their accepted significances from them. His paintings revive the visions of infancy, when the world reveals itself in all its freshness and novelty. However, if they mislead by reason of their revolt against the conventional view of external reality, we cannot affirm that they spring solely from automatism, since, in Picasso's case, "the effort is directed by a totally conscious will, which takes a hand for perhaps the first time." But as this artist has the great merit "of confronting all that exists with all that can exist," there is no need to ask for an account of the means used to tear man from everything conventional. In André Breton's eyes, he is not great so much "because he finds himself so constantly in the position of defense as regards external objects, including those that he takes from himself and that, between the self and the world, he has never kept, as for the moments of mediation. The perishable and the ephemeral, normally on the wrong side of everything that forms an object of delight and artistic vanity, have been sought for the sake of themselves." To appreciate such works, everything in the way of reason, logic, and aesthetic prejudgment must be forgotten.

SURREALISM'S TWO DIRECTIONS—on the one hand its evocation of the mystery of the unconscious, and on the other its disruption of reality—are, then, reconciled in Picasso's work. His revolutionary will distinguishes itself by an entirely characteristic aggressiveness. In contrast, the Surrealist painters differ from each other according to their temperaments: while some especially express their dreams, others throw themselves upon reality in order to restore its profundity.

Artists such as Francis Picabia and Marcel Duchamp adhere to the subjective tendency in Surrealist painting. With them, "We have something that is no longer painting, neither is it even the poetry or philosophy of painting, but what may well be described as the interior landscapes of a man who set out a long time ago for the ultimate pole of his being."

Similarly, an inexpressible quality is released by André Masson's paintings, and, as regards Joan Miro, André Breton has always maintained that he is "the most Surrealist" of all his followers, owing to his total abandon to automatism. "No one is so ready as Miro to associate the inassociable, or to smash unconcernedly what we had not the courage even to wish to see smashed." He makes himself the instrument of those higher powers to which "the great primitive painters have had some little affinity. . . . It is due to these powers that he knows that the earth is drawn across the sky only by the doleful horns of a snail, that the air is a window opening onto a rocket or a huge pair of mustaches . . . that the smoker's mouth is itself formed from smoke, and that the solar spectrum, the painting's promise-maker, announces itself like a spectre, by rattling chains."

Yves Tanguy's pictures also take us into a world of mystery, and make laughable the pretensions of amateur art critics, who want at any cost to recognize in them normal objects, such as animals or trees; the victims, as they can only be, of this tendency to trace the unknown to the known, instead of urging themselves along new roads. Yves Tanguy paints a universe in which the laws of our world are overthrown, in which "the sack of feathers weighs as much as the sack of lead, and in which everything can fly away as easily as it can bury itself."

These painters have an originality that leaves the simple imitators of nature far behind. As in a dream, reality serves only to furnish elements that they organize as their inspiration dictates.

LEONARDO DA VINCI had already insisted upon the importance of the creative imagination for which the artist's synthesis of perceptions is only a springboard for launching into the unreal. "If you take careful note," he told his pupils, "of the soiled patches on ancient walls, or of the mottling of certain quartzes, you will encounter an endless variety of representations—landscapes, the turmoil of battle, spiritual forms, the likenesses of strange heads and figures, fantastic clothes, and an infinity of other things, because the mind is excited by this confusion and finds in it a great wealth of invention." The Surrealist painters, in expressing their inner world, had to do no more than revive this concept and apply it.

Thus, "the whole problem of transition from subjectivity to objectivity" is resolved in Leonardo's lesson instructing his pupils "to copy their pictures from what they will see has painted itself" when they study an ancient wall. According to André Breton, "The scope of this solution far exceeds in human interest that of a technique, when this technique will be compact of inspiration itself." The images thus displayed on a wall, in a shadow, or by any similar means, become the symbols of repressed desires, and the Surrealists always keep faith with their aim—to reveal the

original nature of man by interpreting the signs that manifest it, and this with the purpose of cracking the veneer of
education.

Max Ernst, in describing the genesis of some of his
pictures, affirms this secondary role of the real, which serves
only to substantiate the Surreal:

> Coming at random, or as if at random, upon, for in-
> stance, the pages of a catalogue featuring some objects in-
> tended for anatomical or physiological demonstration, we
> find associated there certain elements that are anatomically
> so remote from each other that the collection's absurdity in-
> duces in us a hallucinatory succession of conflicting images,
> superimposing themselves one upon the other with such
> persistence and speed as would be appropriate for amatory
> reminiscence. The images claim for themselves a new plane
> for their encounter in a new unknown (the plane of non-
> conformity). Then it suffices, by painting or drawing, to de-
> pict the scheme, and for that we need do no more than sub-
> missively reproduce *what reveals itself within us*—a color, a
> scrawl, a strange view of the represented objects, the desert,
> the sky, a geological section, a floor, and a single straight
> line signifying the horizon—in order to obtain a faithful and
> fixed image of our hallucination and transform it into a
> drama revealing our most secret desires, and this from what
> in the first place was only an ordinary page of advertising
> matter.

In that way, Max Ernst was led to invent the technique of *frottage* (rubbing), based on the *intensification of
sensitivity in the mental faculties* induced by placing at

random some sheets of paper coated with powdered
graphite on the surface of the paneled parquetry that
obsesses him. "Through a series of suggestions and trans-
mutations that arise spontaneously, in the manner of
hypnagogic visions, the designs thus obtained increasingly
lose the character of the material in question (the wood),
and assume the aspect of images of unexpected precision—
probably of a nature that reveals the original cause of the
obsession, or that produces a likeness of that cause." By the
same means Ernst exploited various materials, such as
"leaves and their veins, and the unraveled edges of sack-
cloth"; the pictures that resulted he called *Histoire
Naturelle*. He also applied this technique to painting, by
"grating colors onto a base that is colored and placed on an
uneven surface."

The artist, like the clairvoyant who interprets tea
leaves or coffee grounds, endeavors to decipher himself by
means of the symbols in which his unconscious finds expression. These symbols are always the same for a given
person. Their choice, according to André Breton, "betrays
the man," just as do dreams and verbal slips, and it is this
betrayal that concerns Surrealism, this bringing together
of art and psychoanalysis.

The point is not to go on seeing the external world
as it appears to everyone, but to read ourselves by means
of it. This self-reversion is facilitated by fixing the attention
on a single external point, which, by arresting the course
of everyday preoccupations, frees unconscious activity.

Thus, without going as far as hypnotism, "certain isolated images offered us by paintings are capable of fixing the consciousness to the point of making it coincide with them, thereby arresting the external flood of words and impressions, the immense *evasion* that normally forms our consciousness," as Paul Nougé points out.

We do not really put up a resistance to the spirit; but in its case, immobility becomes confused with death. The huge, dark river that rolls unwearyingly in the depths of us breaks all its dams and bursts suddenly into the light, constraining man to see, think, and feel everything he believed himself forever incapable of experiencing or desiring. Thus, the painting's power alone will explain itself. In this we can speak of "illumination" and "revelation."

From self-knowledge, art carries us to knowledge of the universe. That is why Salvador Dali uses "every means to lead us into another world." He throws discredit on everyday reality, and he will even imitate "the unpredictable maneuvers of dreams in order to reverse all the natural laws—those conserving laws whose vision of total immobility can only support the onlooker's formidable inborn lethargy. He will scrupulously decline to put into his pictures objects that it is normal to see associated, but will apply himself to creating the most stupefying and the most *frenzied* encounters."

In Dali's work prior to World War II, this Surrealistic tendency expanded until it overtook the concrete, in Dali's attempt to resolve the conflict between dream and reality.

He interpreted the irrational, not by figures and constructions defying all description, but by representations of real objects, going so far as to make veritable magazine drawings of them. Thus, "The raw object, with its sickly gloss, and its intimate details, in no way obscured by pictorial veils, can carry on with its neighboring object a duologue having the overtones of the infinite." As André Lhote puts it, "Such are the duologues that Dali paints, and his works, as instantaneous as dreams, are achieved with confidence, cruelty, and unsurpassable vitality. Man is compelled either to run away or to collaborate in this magic ceremony, which for a time will pluck him from the ignominy of his virtuous and practical existence." Disoriented, the spirit frees itself from preconceived ideas, like those of morality and shame.

The disturbing power of these canvases is greater by far than that of pictures which simply illustrate dreams, since they directly attack the real world, making its recognizable elements return into chaos. This hallucinatory art, superior to poetry by the precision of its images, brings into being "some absolutely new entities, visibly malevolent."

THIS PROPENSITY for intertwining the subjective and the objective conforms to the evolution of Surrealism, which sought to enrich the reality from which it had itself originally turned away. Paintings that are, above all, subjective, such as those of Miro and Tanguy, concur only in Surrealism's first aspect, which, although certainly essential, is by itself incomplete. The Surrealists therefore adopted the Cubist technique of collage, so that they could bring themselves still closer to this sought-after unity. Thanks to the use of ready-made elements "it became possible"—wrote Max Morise—"for the painter to make a cinematographic exposure of his thought at every second." By means of this new language he could express his inner dynamism as rapidly as the poet.

Thus it is the cinema that ought to offer the maximum possibilities to the Surrealists: first, because it operates in the dimension of time, thus reproducing the behavior of thought, and second, because it is composed of objective photographs that, thanks to montage, enable the fantastic to be integrated with the real, thus restoring to reality its profundity. Unfortunately, there are few Surrealist films.

In *L'Age d'Or,* made by Bunuel and Dali in 1930, we witness a hallucinatory succession of images. Max Ernst has listed some of them: "The cow in the bed, the bishop and the giraffe thrown from the window, the dung-cart crossing the governor's drawing room, the Minister for the Interior stuck to the ceiling after his suicide." As in *Le Chien Andalou,* another Surrealist film, everyday reality is turned upside down by the expression of tendencies repressed by the individual. Thus, worldly images of love and desire superimpose themselves upon those of a life that is strait-laced and monotonous.

Such films, however, have reached only an extremely

limited public, and the Surrealists, therefore, have had to be content to translate their dreams by the use of photographs and engravings, the ready-made materials of this "painting without pencil or paints." From the assembling of these materials a picture results, in the same way as, for the Surrealists, a poem springs from the juxtaposition of newspaper headlines. According to Max Ernst, the most noble conquest here would be that of the *irrational*, and in his collages "he endeavored, *with the help of the image, to establish between the beings and the things—thought of as the data—other relationships than the ones that establish themselves ordinarily and, as it were, provisionally.*"

In a comparable way it was in order to suggest Surreality that Man Ray, by new photographic techniques, succeeded in effecting a veritable transformation of his negatives.

Thus photographs, faithful reproductions of ordinary objects, can serve, either by improvised rearrangement or by transformation, to propel the mind toward subjectivity. As in Salvador Dali's paranoiac-critical method, the world's given data are considered in relation to the subject, not for practical ends, but solely to induce inner visions. The experimental objects represented by the photographs or incorporated in the pictures are not displayed for their own sakes, but serve as toys in the painter's hands for the expression of his unconscious. He not only externalizes his dreams, but makes them share in a reality that seems commonplace until he restores its mystery. "The 'that-isn't-painting' of the public only proves to him the colossal reality of stuck-on paper, the Surreality of collage."

This tendency may be noted in Picasso, who sprinkles sand or sticks paper onto his pictures. Art should be so little subjugated to the means of expression that Picabia considers that beauty can be born from the combination of the most unexpected materials, provided the hand that assembles them is an artist's hand. To prove this to a skeptic, he made a picture representing a village of the Midi in which confetti flowers strew a lawn on which grow trees that have macaroni for their trunks and feathers for their leaves, while the treads of a flight of steps are made of straw placed horizontally. Thus, the essential element is inspiration, not technique, and the genuine artist can express his vision irrespective of the means employed.

As Tristan Tzara has written: "The differences between materials, which the eye can convert into tactile sensation, give new depths to a picture in which weight suggests itself with mathematical precision by means of symbols standing for volume, density, consistency, and even the taste of the picture's materials on the tongue—these factors confront us with a matchless reality in a world created by the force of the mind and the dream."

The artist allies himself with the metaphysician in his endeavors to liberate the vision, to harness the imagination to nature, to consider everything that is possible as real, and to show us that there is no division between Surreality and reality, from the standpoint of an Absolute that encompasses them both.

Architecture

This conception of art had a powerful influence on decoration and on sculpture, particularly as regards Alberto Giacometti and Hans Arp, whose wooden cutouts evoked "silhouettes of another world." In architecture, the Surrealists' predilections took them toward the modern style, the undulating lines and formal intricacies of which recall the sinuousness of shapes seen in dreams.

André Breton related this style to works executed by mediums, or under the influence of automatism alone. Thus, a simple postman called Cheval, in total ignorance of the principles of architecture, constructed nothing less than a "dream palace," which can be seen at Hautes-Rives in the department of Drôme. This postman brought a stone back from each of his rounds and, by placing it on his folly, succeeded in raising an edifice the complicated and tortuous lines of which recall those of a Buddhist temple.

Such constructions signal "the triumph of the equivocal . . . , of the complex," by their borrowing of "motifs from the vegetable world and from the ancient arts of Asia and Mexico." According to Salvador Dali, no "collective effort creates a world so pure, and also so disturbing, as these modern-style buildings, which, on the border of architecture, constitute true representations of realized desires in which the cruelest and most violent automatism gloomily demonstrates hatred of reality and the need to take refuge in an imaginary world, just as happens in infantile neurosis."

This style, the monuments of which reveal "a concrete irrationality," developed in spite of everything between the two wars. Indeed, a room with "irrationally wavy" walls, although accounted "outside all the conditions of rationality and plainness," was proposed for the Swiss Pavilion of the University City, and André Breton opposed its critics from his own standpoint: "This magnificent church, done entirely in the vegetables and shellfish of Barcelona."

As André Lhote points out, this preoccupation with labyrinthine curves and whiplash flourishes is found in the art of "Picasso, Braque, Lipchitz, Masson, and Dali, in whose eyes even the entrance to the Métro evokes, by its tangled forms, the discoveries and fascinations of their younger days."

In architecture, as in the other arts, the point always is to express the sinuous rhythms of thought in opposition to fixed laws and to all traces of arid logic.

Theatre

No province of art is foreign territory to the Surrealists, whose spirit is to be found at the source of all original manifestations, the more so as, under the pressure of psychological crisis, they increasingly interest themselves in displays that show life in its unfamiliar aspects. Albert Thibaudet can even write, "We go to the theatre as we go to the surgeon or the dentist," so great is its hold on the audience.

Alfred Jarry had an immense influence on the modern theatre. By giving small importance to reality, and drunk with a freedom that encouraged him to express all his fantasies, he opened the door to anarchy and individualism. *Ubu Roi* achieved a *succès de scandale,* but it was not of its times, and, as Marcel Schwob pointed out, "The public invited to see 'its ignoble alter ego' will prefer to extract from the play a moral lecture on abuses."

The better to display his destructive intentions, Jarry followed with *Ubu Enchainé,* dealing with the individual reduced to slavery by collective life; the play was not produced until thirty years after Jarry's death, when Père Ubu's adventures unfolded themselves in the midst of Max Ernst's décor, which was composed of photogravures in the style of his collages, and which had the effect of increasing still more the confusion already created by the play's humor.

This trend, which consisted of illuminating reality by showing up its absurdities, was revived by Apollinaire, and it was he who coined the word "Surrealist," to describe his drama *Les Mamelles de Tirésias.* Its première took place on June 24, 1917, and in it the most surprising scenes followed one another, while its characters appeared to say and do everything their fantasy dictated.

Such works are little appreciated by the public, which

prefers murder mysteries and does not much care to see itself in its true guise. Although the dramatists who embellish the facts of human existence and dissemble our real motives meet with easy success, "the gramophone," that rather unexpected and comic character in *Mariés de la Tour Eiffel*, infuriates the audience, which refuses to recognize the play's wedding guests as its contemporaries, and deplores their words and gestures. For all that, Jean Cocteau has proved his courage by looking things in the face, because, as Pirandello has showed, man holds so strongly to his illusions that when they are revealed to him as being illusions, he seems at once to lose his reasons for living, and sinks into near-neurosis.

Naturally, many theatregoers do not trouble to look further than the clown's antics, since with theatre, as with music and all the other arts, originality always attracts abuse. "Booing, catcalls, and applause. Shocking press. A few surprising notices. Three years later the play's detractors applaud, and don't remember that they ever booed. That's the history of *Parade*, and of every play that changes the rules of the game."

In keeping with these breaks with tradition, the Russian ballet has indeed introduced some new rhythms, sharing the spirit of innovation that characterized the start of the twentieth century. Sergei Diaghilev helped to spread these tendencies. After the *Sacre du Printemps, Parade*, produced in 1917, was his war cry. Hardly stopping for breath, he passed from the stage of primitive life to that of the machine age, danced to Erik Satie's music and against décor by Picasso. Diaghilev certainly had a great appeal, not only to the musicians but also to the avant-garde painters. Cubists such as Braque, Derain, and Juan Gris, and Surrealists such as Chirico and Miro, created dazzling scenic designs for his ballets, in which the dancers' costumes completed the enchanted pattern of colors.

THE RUSSIAN BALLET, by achieving the union of dance, music, and painting, reminded the spectator of his dreams' subtle associations. Moreover, some Surrealists, such as Pierre-Albert Birot, and above all, Antonin Artaud, believed that the reform of the theatre ought to include production. About 1918, Birot wrote a sort of "polydrama," *Le Bondieu,* which was to have been acted by a multitude of characters performing on two superimposed sets. On one of them, the actors, dressed in symbolic costumes, were to have worn masks. One of the principals, Sovkipeu, would have been installed in a kind of coffin made of black wood, in which there would have been a little shutter at head-level that he could open and close. Each member of the chorus would have worn a single tunic with an opening for his head, while the rest of the garment would have hung as straight as a sleeve. In contrast, the actors on the other set were to have been in street clothes.

The production's spaciousness had a much deeper significance than that of simply providing a spectacle. It intended nothing less than to carry the audience toward the absolute. As in Oriental drama, "This compact collection of gestures, signs, attitudes, and sounds comprises the language of the production and the set, and this language, promoting its physical and poetic consequences on all planes of consciousness, and in all the senses, necessarily conduces thought to adopt profound inflections, which can be described as *metaphysics in action.*" In fact, for Antonin Artaud, the theatre's true purpose is "to interpret life from a large and universal point of view, and to extract from this life images that we would be delighted to encounter again." The theatre ought to be

> thought of as the duplicate, not of this everyday and obvious reality—a representation that would gradually dwindle to no more than a lifeless copy, as pointless as over-sweet—but the double of another reality, one that is formidable and authentic, in which principals, like dolphins, show their heads above water, then eagerly return to the depths. This latter reality is not human, but inhuman, and in it man, with his morality and his character, counts, it must be said, for extremely little.

Of the Western theatre, Antonin Artaud makes the same criticisms that André Breton levels at those allegedly psychological novels the descriptions of emotions in which are without interest because authentic life is absent. The theatre should take the spectator back into that world of dreams and instincts that is "sanguinary and cruel." What matters is to impress the senses, since they are inseparable from the understanding. "I propose," writes Artaud, "to awaken the theatre with that concept of primitive magic, revived by modern psychoanalysis, that consists in curing a patient by having him adopt the external attributes of the condition from which he is to be reclaimed." A work that expresses the forces repressed in a man frees him from them, and, in the same way, the theatrical production that enchants its audience by formative means, will, so to speak, induce a hypnotic trance. "Only the East has been able to provide the theatre with a physical and nonverbal concept, in which the drama is contained within the limits of everything that can take place on a set, independently of the written text, in contrast to the theatre as we know it in the West, where the drama is partly bound to the text, and finds itself limited by it." In the West, the theatre is thought of as a part of literature, whereas, for instance, the Balinese spectacle is addressed to the whole being, and its lines have the force of incantations. "Once and for all, it breaks the theatre's intellectual subjugation to language by giving it a new and deeper sense of intellectuality, which, hiding under the gestures and signs, raises it to the dignity of a specific exorcism."

Antonin Artaud elaborated a complete technique of dramatic representation. "The spectator is at the center, and the spectacle surrounds him," so that he shares the same atmosphere as the actors. Sounds, noises, and cries will be employed according to their vibratory qualities, lighting will be used according to the effect of the different colors on the organic whole. The display of images in their concrete aspects will be effected by actors wearing enormous masks. The action will tend to be violent, since "everything that moves is cruel," and the theatre, seeking to express life, will be like a torrent carrying everything with it on its course.

"Blood and violence having been made to serve the violence of thought," the spectator, purged of his murderous and rapacious instincts, is incapable "of surrendering himself to external ideas of war, riot, or assassination." The theatre thus exercises "an exceptional power of diversion," which, according to Antonin Artaud, is particularly necessary in an age of demoralization such as that we live in. Such a spectacle is far from being a psychological analysis of the passions, since it ought to equate itself "to a sort of liberated life that cleanses human individuality and in which man is no longer only a reflection."

So, for us in the West, art, the mission of which should be to explain the riches of the infinite, is completely divorced from life. "The spiritual sickness of the West, which is pre-eminently the place where art is confused with aestheticism, is to think that a painting is only a picture, and a dance only an expression of formal movement, as if it were desirable to separate the various art forms, and to cut the bonds that link them to the mystical attitudes in which they can confront the absolute."

THE SURREALISTS, by employing art as the language of the ineffable, have done no more than express their true goal. The artist is always an inspired being who shows us a new aspect of the world, even when he departs from nature. Thus André Breton was able to draw up a list of writers, starting with Edward Young and Dean Swift, taking in Poe, Baudelaire, and Rimbaud, and concluding with Pierre Reverdy, Saint-John Perse, and Raymond Roussel, all of whom were Surrealists in some respects. Only "a certain number of preconceived ideas they held" prevented them from constantly sharing "the Surrealist voice, that voice which preaches unfalteringly above the storm and from dawn to death."

This dispassionate search for another reality inherent in art is more or less dissembled beneath rational appearances, but when it becomes aware of itself it develops in all its amplitude, and the poets no longer trouble to reveal their intuitions in a form comprehensible to all. Torn by the disquiet imparted by the limits of the human condition, they seek only to fathom the mystery through visions that carry them far from the real.

German Romanticism was an impassioned effort to snatch the secret of the universe. Its poets found that their inner life was only the reflection of the cosmos, and by means of the one they endeavored to fuse themselves with the other. Whereas the French Romantics remained at the stage of pure subjectivism, they strove to identify the subjective and the objective in a supreme unity.

The self ended by vanishing before this Infinite of which it is only the emanation. According to André Breton, "The whole history of thought since Joachim von Arnim is one of liberties taken with this idea of 'I am,' which is beginning to be lost in itself." As an example, Breton quotes Rimbaud's profession of philosophical faith: "It is wrong to say: 'I think.' One should say: 'Someone thinks me.' . . . The 'I' is someone else."

Art is an authentic experience that, from a point beyond understanding, seeks to attain to metaphysical certainty. As Novalis wrote, "Poetry is the real made absolute." To consider the world of visible realities as the symbol of an invisible world, or to think of a frozen world of ideas as trying to make itself equal to plunging into its own abysses, are only different ways of attaining the unknowable.

3 / The Surrealist Synthesis

The Metamoral Aspect

"If it were not for the Poetic or Prophetic character, the Philosophic and Experimental would soon be at the ratio of all things, and stand still, unable to do other than repeat the same dull round over again."* This observation of William Blake's, quoted by Paul Eluard, especially applies to impassioned seekers after truth. The revelation is only granted to them because they have risen above their limited horizons.

People who evade society's normal values in their endeavor to reach the ineffable experience that challenge which Bergson says is no more than a conquest of con-

* From the text of the "There Is No Natural Religion" etchings. (First series.)

sciousness by "the life force," which incites "the open soul" to escape its limits; and it is this challenge that makes artists and heroes seek to fathom their unconscious that they may communicate with this total life of which they have some presentiment. "It is living and ceasing to live that are the imaginary interludes," says André Breton. "Existence is something else entirely."

Poets and mystics start, then, by dying, so to speak— by leaving the everyday world. They surrender themselves to inspiration, and slip into the mists, drawn by the light of fascination shining from the farther side. Certainly it was by way of sleep's shadows that Gérard de Nerval hoped to become one with the ultimate reality, and certainly it was a "shadowy unity" that Baudelaire aspired to.

The Surrealists, at the start of their researches, thought of themselves as receptacles, as echoes of what "some were tempted to take for universal consciousness." Tormented by a thirst for the absolute that religion could no longer quench, "They remained confident in Rimbaud's mighty pledge, awaiting, as he had awaited, the nameless visitation," as Jacques Rivière puts it. "Meanwhile, they worked unceasingly, with even more zeal and tenacity than their predecessors, to induce attendances of the unknown among them and to secure whatever elements there are that prowl all confines of the spirit."

This seems a long way from literature and art. What was important was no longer to express or even to transform reality, but to surpass it and reach a world invisible to mortal eyes. "Poetry, then, should be termed an assembly of phenomena to which some brains are subject, just as mediums are subject to supernatural occurrences. The notation of these phenomena should be comparable in every way to the written accounts of séances." Moreover, adds Jacques Rivière, the Surrealists' insistence "upon recommending to us the works of nonprofessional writers, like idiots or unconscious subjects" is significant of "the Surrealists' only religion—belief in the mystic—and of their constant expectation of a poetic visitation of the spirit [*d'une Pentecôte poétique*]."

The most unexpected verbal associations, Chirico's early pictures, Man Ray's photographs, "in which a pair of compasses, a pencil, and a set-square waltz together until a fabulous light falls upon their gyrations and transfigures them, are no more than a means of escaping all aesthetic appreciation by diverting the mind toward some *noumenon*."

In this sense, Surrealism is firmly opposed to the subjectivism of Romanticism, in which, as in Impressionism, the self serves simply as a passageway. The techniques of Surrealism are no more than ways of achieving the effacement of the personality in order to gain a cosmic consciousness. The "exquisite corpse" procedure, by the reactions it stimulates between minds, liberates them to their limits. Certain poems, such as *Ralentir Travaux*, by André Breton, Paul Eluard, and René Char, illustrate Lautréamont's axiom that "poetry ought to be made by all"—the sheet of white paper being only "the meeting place of a great number of consciousnesses, as aspects of a single consciousness." Thus, "The characteristic of Surrealism is to proclaim the total equality of all human beings in face of the subliminal message, and to maintain unremittingly that this message constitutes a common heritage of which each of us should demand no more than his share, and which must very soon cease to be considered the prerogative of a minority."

Thus, each Surrealist work has an importance that both infinitely exceeds and runs counter to that rationality which narrows our minds beyond hope. For some, the world of the unconscious assumes such importance that the world near at hand seems no more than a fading screen. The practice of automatism and the surrender to spontaneity, by leading the individual to lose his conception of a limited self, brings Surrealism close to Oriental thought, which, indeed, aims at destroying the ego and at rescuing the self from all egotistic feeling, so that it can merge in the supreme reality. André Breton is at one with Count Keyserling when the latter defines this metaphysical concept: "This concept does not speak of an existence in which God, the world, and the soul are reunited, or of one that is the purest essence of total multiplicity; it is no more than a concept of unalloyed intensity, it aims only at life itself, this *in-objective* whence things arise as from incidents."

The Surrealist, in expressing the absolute, feels he has a mission to achieve. "All we know," writes André Breton again, "is that to some extent we are endowed with the gift of words, and that, by means of it, something immense and obscure endeavors to express itself through us; and that each of us has been chosen as one out of a thousand, and designated to formulate by himself what, in our lifetimes, must be formulated. It is an order we have been given, once and for all, and it has never occurred to us to dispute it."

ALL WAYS, those of the flesh as much as those of abnegation, can lead to this absolute that lies beyond good and evil. At the fork of the roads, leading either to God or to the Devil, some take the "narrow way," whereas others plunge into the "forbidden zone." But whatever route be taken, or whatever nature be attributed to unity, whether spiritual or material, it is always the same force that impels all of us.

For the Surrealists who formed the *Grand Jeu* group,

A man can, with the help of certain techniques, called "mystic," attain an immediate perception of another universe that is immeasurable by his senses and irreducible by his understanding; and awareness of this universe marks an intermediary stage between individual consciousness and the other kind. This stage is shared by all those who, at some period of their lives, have wished desperately to go beyond the inherent possibilities of their species, and have anticipated in outline what lies beyond mortality.

It is in this sense that Marcel Raymond considers that

> Of all the philosophic concepts, that of esoteric thought, handed down and enriched by a multisecular tradition, seems to present the least difficulty as regards achieving accord with Surrealism. Forbodings concerning another, super-real, universe, which incorporates the subjective and the objective, the internal and the external, and from which messages can be received by "letting the senses die" . . . seem to be the most normal consequence of the denial of the Surrealists and their latent mysticism.

Yet how much more tempting for the rebels is the adventure of ransacking hell to appease their thirst for the infinite. The blasphemies of pretended atheists fundamentally only express not so much the negation of God as dissatisfaction with the too human concept of God evolved by their contemporaries. As Pierre Klossovsky points out, it was only by profaning religious symbols that the Marquis de Sade, far from being indifferent to religion, could "overcome his apparent atheism," and again, it was out of hostility to popular moral values that Baudelaire sang the beauties of evil, and Rimbaud, aspiring to an ideal purity, shocked those same values by his blasphemies. This same abhorrence made Lautréamont defy the Creator in his *Les Chants de Maldoror*, and it now urges the Surrealists to descend by means of low practices toward "the world of true realities—of Surrealities, which, contrary to the Platonic hypotheses, are not formed from ideas, and still less are, as Descartes would have it, formed from evident ideas, for there is nothing less intellectual than Surreality in all existence." Was it not "by studying the bodily senses" that Antonin Artaud hoped to arrive at a metaphysics of the state of being, at the definitive knowledge of life? And Pierre-Jean Jouve was not able to release himself from "the earthly aspect of Error." Engulfing himself in sin, surrendering himself to his libido, the veritable "God in hell" will offer a road toward freedom, toward the Paradise Lost.

The existence of another reality placed either in the world of ideas or in that of the instincts is proved by a mental exercise—the argument of reminiscence—that can apply to either of these glimpsed worlds. André Breton states: "It has happened to me to use, in a Surrealist connection, some words the meanings of which I had forgotten. Afterward I was able to verify that the sense I had given them corresponded exactly to their dictionary definitions. This leads to the belief that we do not learn, that we never do more than *re-learn*."

THE TWO ROADS by which man can travel in quest of the absolute result from the duality of his nature, standing, as it does, at a point midway between spirituality and animalism. If he is not saved by grace "he will live in a state of hopeless rebellion, in a perpetual paradox; he desperately desires to be himself, not a feeble emanation of himself, but so fully himself that he makes of himself a horrible god. In his demoniacal rage man, abhorring life, desires to be himself in all his horror and through this torment to protest against all life."

Kierkegaard indeed expresses most graphically the anguish of the consciousness that, by impelling itself into subjectivity, collides with the transcendence of this "other" that dwells within it, since, as Jean Wahl points out, "The passion that makes us touch bottom in the inner consciousness brings us into contact with an external entity." Thus, man feels himself seized by a sort of vertigo in his ignorance of the nature of this "other," and while—in contrast to the mystics—he dreads to descend into himself, he will remain his own prisoner. It is this that makes Robert Desnos exclaim: "I don't believe in God, but I have a sense of the Infinite. No one has a more religious spirit than me. I hurl myself ceaselessly at insoluble questions, and the questions that I have to resolve are all insoluble."

Those artists whose lives have been constantly torn apart by those two concepts, that of subjectivity and that of transcendence, make us aware of existence's profundity far better than a purely didactic account. The formulation of a theory may be the mark of a philosophic spirit, but to live intensely allows the fullest attainment of life's very roots. Thus, the originality of Surrealism is in its simultaneous passing beyond the plane of the aesthetic and that of a uniquely speculative philosophy. From that point of view, it orients itself toward the thought of the great Indian sages, who teach that we can only truly understand what we can make real.

MANY WERE THOSE, however, who, by dashing themselves against this barrier that divided them from the ultimate ecstasy, were to sink into madness or otherwise lose all touch with this world, since the poet, even if he succeeds in transcending himself, can be thrown into fresh despair when he feels himself powerless to interpret the transcendent, and finds that poetry's metaphysical aspirations have led him up a blind alley. "Poetry, which is all creation, and which is nothing without expression, is compelled to expound an absolute renouncing all expression. Is not this contradictory?" And perhaps it was because he could not surmount this contradiction that Arthur Rimbaud retreated into silence, and that Germain Nouveau—whom the Surrealists also claim for themselves—advanced into asceticism.

That poetic experience can excite its votaries as far as mysticism does not change the fact that the mystic aspires to silence while "the poet makes his way toward utterance." If he is able to express his vision, he recovers his inner balance, but if he feels that his vision is betrayed by his language, he is rent by that conflict which Antonin Artaud nakedly displays in his *Correspondance avec Jacques Rivière*. He writes: "I suffer from an appalling sickness of the spirit. Thought deserts me at every level—from thought as a simple fact to thought as an external fact materialized in words. . . . I plumb the depths of myself, I know it, I suffer from it, but I acquiesce from fear of dying altogether."

Artaud's poetry makes us feel that it is genuinely and

intensely true to life, that it expresses the most profound depths of his nature. For many, literature is only an intellectual game, but for Artaud it blends with his aspiration toward the immutable. He wants to attain the closest secrets of himself, to escape from the prison of his body into conditions beyond space and time, but he cannot lose himself in the Absolute, although it is just such crises that will cause a mystic to submerge himself in God.

In short, the desperate poet, under the spell of the demoniac, never obtains a certainty comparable to that of the mystic, who, in his explorations of what is within, is constantly supported by his faith. It is only by means of groping through a darkness made up of despair and backsliding that the poet eventually emerges to the splendors of an indefinable light, and so has the impression of being "the thief of fire."

THE SURREALISTS' earliest discoveries concerning the action of the unconscious made them hope that, by giving themselves up to automatism, they would reach the very roots of existence. As Jacques and Raissa Maritain point out:

> Trapped by an experience they could no longer ignore, but opposed in general to all religious forms and even to the idea of God, they only wanted to discover the sources of poetry, and they invested poetry with the duties of sanctity, although they lacked the means of sanctity, which are es-

sentially self-given. They encumbered poetry with this bur-
den at the start, and later, when it did not give them what
they expected, they underestimated it. And then, a fresh
despair hurled them into other spiritual adventures.

Many roads lead to the divine state, but all must reach
as far as the final goal: fusion in the Grand Totality. If
the Surrealists' original rebellion drove them to question
themselves as to the nature of the "beyond," it nevertheless
had to be in relation to this life, for the Surreal is not the
supernatural. Their resistance to this infatuation, of which
Gérard de Nerval was a victim, made them condemn the
Grand Jeu group, refusing to let themselves be captivated
by this descent into the self, from which people often fail
to return.

The exploration of the lower depths of psychology,
of the "under-real," undertaken in the beginning as a pro-
vocative gesture against morality, should subsequently
enable man to become aware of his possibilities. It is not
enough, as Robert Desnos believed, for man to become the
instrument of his unconsciousness, for he should occupy
himself with finding a concrete solution to the problems of
existence. Surreality is not to be sought solely on "the other
side," but should become integrated with the attributes of
consciousness in order to recognize this harmony of being
that will finally reconcile man to himself.

If at the start of their investigations the Surrealists
impelled themselves to the conquest of the absolute—of a

Surreality that they placed in this world—they later overcame their anguished desire for the Infinite and turned from its inscrutable mysteries. Then they oriented themselves toward Freud, who looked upon our inner life as the key to events that were certainly terrestrial but apparently inexplicable.

The Surreal was no longer the absolute, but a concept correlated to the real, and psychoanalysis had lowered it from the transcendent to what is inherent. The Surrealists then endeavored to make a synthesis of these two contradictory aspects of the world. Surreality became "the spiritual point where life and death, the real and the imaginary, the past and the future, the communicable and the incommunicable, the high and the low, ceased to be seen contradictorily." The Surrealists' fundamental aim is still this search for total unity, but far from placing it evasively in a supraterrestrial area, they try to achieve it in the world of facts. They return to the real—which once they rebelled against—enriched by their discoveries. Marxism is the result of this return to the concrete, since it encourages their hope of reconciling man with those two elements of his being—consciousness and the unconscious —between which present-day society serves only to artificially accentuate the conflict.

This evolution of Surrealism can be illustrated by an inverted cone, the base of which represents metaphysics, the apex Marxism, and the area in between psychoanalysis.

The Psychoanalytic Aspect

Freud, the inventor of psychoanalysis, used it to confront man with himself in a state of terrifying nakedness, and with the mask of his smug and hypocritical image lifted to reveal his baseness and ignominy. He rejected man's social veneer, and stripped away the appearance of civilization. In his opinion, sexual desire was the chief driving force of man, and man should look it squarely in the face and not delude himself, taking refuge in a sterile skepticism or confusing himself with worthless theories.

André Breton, for his part, was not only a poet, but wanted as well to build a doctrine of life and to be a leader of men, in order to counteract this drift toward nihilism, which all too often engendered a tendency in man to grow inward upon himself. If, for a start, he sought to escape from the world, it was only to enable him the better to put himself in his true place as a result, and to benefit from his adventures into the unknown lands of the subconscious.

Psychoanalysis, by depriving this unrecognized field of the vital forces of its occult character, can only satisfy Surrealism's positive aim, that is, its endeavor to integrate the irrational with the rational. Then it reassumes a psychological aspect, and in André Breton's *Premier Manifeste*, he defines it in this way: "Pure psychological automatism is the means by which it is proposed to express the real func-

tioning of thought, whether verbally or in writing or by
any other method at all. The material is dictated by thought
in the absence of all control exerted by reason, and outside
all aesthetic and moral considerations." This process is
presented as an experimental and scientific endeavor to
explore the unconscious, in which Surreality dwells. A
"Bureau de Recherches Surréalistes" will be set up with a
view to collecting all "related communications in the
various forms that the mind's unconscious behavior is
susceptible to. No particular sphere is specified a priori for
this enterprise, and the Surrealist movement simply proposes
to assemble the greatest possible amount of experimental
data, for a purpose that cannot yet be foreseen." In that
way archives would be constituted containing the replies
to the various inquiries conducted by the *Révolution Surréaliste* on "all the special conditions under which the mind
functions in isolation," the mind itself being "totally oblivious of all the inhibitions normally imposed upon it by
the conventions; those, for instance, relating to dreams or
madness or love," in which states "the pure image offers
itself to the brain." Their importance is comprehensive, as
one of them, extracted from the review's twelfth number,
shows:

I. We live in the midst of the apparent. The tangible
universe has but one face, and it is hard for us to surmise
any other. At certain moments in life, after illness or, in particular, mental states, our consciousness has a vision of

things completely *other*. What is the value of this other perception?

II. In such opportunities as we are given of leaving our normal personalities, we can distinguish *physical states:* nervous disorders of the personality, the senses, or the memory, and their consequences—dreams, sleep-walking, madness, visions, hallucinations, supranormal perception, and so forth. What connection have these *phantoms* with *things?* Are they more real, as real, unreal?

III. Besides this "disorganization of the perceptible" there is a "disorganization of the mental qualities"—another reality (although, of course, there is only one reality) accessible by means of passion and inspiration. What connection has the reality that displays itself to us in that way to the rational constructions of consciousness?

The analytical study of such questions helps us toward knowledge of the unconscious mind and its complexes, which then not only cease to torture man below the level of his consciousness but also enable him to know himself far more completely.

Maine de Biran, by reacting against associationist psychology, was the first to draw attention to the profundity of the psychological life, but it was, above all, William James, Henri Bergson, and Pierre Janet who analyzed its dynamism.

Consciousness is only the superficial aspect of a life that unfolds far below the surface; according to Bergson's comparison, our manifest ideas are "like dead leaves on the surface of a pond." It was Freud, however, who extended this discovery of an inner life still further, and disclosed the world of repressed instincts that haunt the individual. The Ego has deep roots, since behind it is found the Self, which is properly the psyche and which belongs to the domain of the unconscious. An article in *La Révolution Surréaliste* entitled "The Question of Analysis by Lay People" explains the difference. "In the Self there is no conflict —in it contradictory and opposite terms associate without confusion, and frequently matters are accommodated by compromise." Whereas the Ego is distinguished by a "remarkable impulse toward unity and synthesis, a characteristic that is lacking in the Self, which is, so to speak, subdivided and without cohesion, so that each of the aspirations it contains pursues its own end without regard to the others." Therefore it is certainly the source of those unforeseen shocks delivered by the characteristic images of Surrealist art.

The Ego lies at the intersection of the outer and inner worlds, and in respect of them finds itself between the hammer and the anvil. The external world is made up of material objects perceptible to the senses, but psychological facts, interpreted by the imagination, are the elements—equally real, if not more so—of the subjective world. "Once again, what attribute of the visual field is it that sheds a melancholy light by physical means, so that no element in a picture has been considered independently of it for a very long time?" André Breton asks himself, apropos of an exhibition of paintings. "And what quality of the visual field, closely related to the first, is it that—due to the texture or propensity of a responsive organ such as the human eye, which is almost as stupid as a chameleon's—affects adversely the ceaseless passing scene? . . . this field in which are scattered in accordance with the least publicized psychological laws all the artist's thought—the artist, this man committed to his afflatus and his personal daemon, hidden, lurking, unwittingly subject to diverse tendencies, multi-intentional, and, in spite of himself, deceiving the social body that harbors him while he communes, alone or not, or with one he loves, as the case may be, in times and places entirely different from all others and, as a matter of course, with visitors normally as little likely to be found together as Henrietta Maria of England, the shadow of an enormous horsetail, and a wasp-waisted diabolo."

This double life has the effect of dispersing man's energies, whereas, for their full spiritual flowering, they should be unified. Nevertheless, this harrowing of the subsoil of the human soul does not take place without disturbing a number of preconceived ideas. Indeed, the inner life takes on much the same sacred character as the phenomena of the external world have for primitive peoples. An analogous anxiety seizes those courageous enough to attempt to illuminate their inner mysteries, just as once seized the astronomer who dared to demonstrate that the stars were not gods. Of course, an immense objectivity and an absolute lack of prejudices are necessary to secure a

manifestation of this "other side" of consciousness. Yet it is
this "other side" that springs up spontaneously in the
course of violent emotions, or under psychoanalysis, just
as it can be stimulated experimentally by the various Surrealist techniques. Nevertheless, extreme hardihood is de-
manded in risking the adventure, and perhaps the Surrealist poet responds to the wish formulated by Jung when
he wrote: "I can imagine myself to be someone urged by a
pseudoreligious curiosity to use such a technique—an
adolescent, for instance, who wants wings, not because he is
paralyzed, but because he has a nostalgic longing for the
sun."

YET IT IS very difficult to tear oneself from the importunities
of the external world in order to retreat into the Self.
Solitude is painful, men seek to consort with others as much
as possible, and they allow themselves to be swallowed up
by those numerous activities that take them out of themselves.

According to Freud, the education of a man represses
his fundamental instincts. Thus, he establishes within himself something like "censorship," which induces conformity
in people, and enables them to live together in the same
society without discomfort. Then all their dynamism takes
refuge in the unconsciousness of their desires.

This censorship is so strong that even the instincts in
their own sphere of activity are not displayed in all their

crudity but, to escape from a rigorous control, disguise themselves behind symbols. More or less identical in every individual, they lend themselves to grandiose myths of a cosmic character. Since the Self is the most primitive basis in human existence, attributes of an ancestral order are to be found within it. According to Freud, "Our existing perception of Self is only the stunted part of a vast, even universal perception, taking the form of a more intimate relationship between the Self and the surrounding world." Thus, psychoanalysis makes explicit this analogy between the microcosm and the macrocosm of which poets already had a presentiment.

In the normal state, the unconscious is content to manifest itself in ways to which the majority of people pay no attention, but if during an individual's development the repressions have been too violent, then the Self has its revenge in the form of a multitude of neuroses, which spell ruin to all balance between the external and internal worlds.

Freud, to his lasting credit, showed that mental troubles have a psychological origin, and that cures could be effected by making the patient conscious of the unsatisfactory trend, or by reproducing the circumstances in which the repression had taken place. It usually happens that an incident is recalled from the patient's most distant past. "The whole of humanity has long since rejected as being contrary to civilization such matters as pleasure in killing, incest, rape, and all those somber excesses of the barbarian hordes, but the desire to repeat these things stirs once again during infancy, that prehistoric epoch of the human soul; and every individual symbolically renews the whole history of civilization in his own ethic development."

Here again we come upon that concept of "cruelty" toward which Antonin Artaud intuitively aimed, and on which he took his stand for the rejuvenation of the theatre. "I use the word 'cruelty,'" he wrote, "as meaning appetite for life, cosmic order, and implacable necessity. I use it in the gnostic sense, as meaning the whirlpool of life that engulfs the darkness, and as meaningless agony beyond ineluctable necessity which life need not inflict; the good is a thing of the will, the result of an act, but evil is permanent."

The psychoanalytical method, then, consists of freeing the unconscious with the aim of identifying the factor that, by erupting into the consciousness despite "censorship," caused the loss of equilibrium. The first indications of the individual's true desires were deduced from the analysis of slips of the tongue and pen, and of failures in behavior, but it is the interpretation of dreams that remains one of the best means of investigation. Indeed, no realm can offer greater riches than that of the dream—a realm in which restraints no longer harass the patient and images are the symbols of the buried life of the instincts. The Surrealists endeavored to decipher dreams by thinking of them in two different ways: either as the results of previous happenings, or as the causes of events that followed them and that seemed fortuitous.

Art, like the accounts of dreams, is one of the signs that express the unconscious, since it reflects the soul's mystery and that of the world. The fact that each artist always employs one particular symbol rather than another shows what André Breton calls the "personality of choice," and by it he reveals a self lying far below the surface. Since each way of interpreting the Surreal reveals one of its aspects, none should be neglected. And the "language of revelation speaks for itself, speaking some words very high, some very low, and from many directions at once. We must resign ourselves to learning that language by bits and pieces."

THE SURREALISTS recapture a concept dear to Freud when they endeavor to show that every phenomenon, no matter what, has a final purpose, and that chance is apparent rather than real, since at the root of any action that seems coincidental, analysis will reveal a motivating desire. André Breton, in *Nadja, Les Vases Communicants,* and *L'Amour Fou,* gives numerous examples of behavior explained by dreams or by past actions. Thus there is a limited interpenetration between natural necessity, which reigns in the external world, and human necessity, which often succeeds in making real the individual's deep inclinations. In the dream, everything happens according to the dreamer's intimate desires, but its materials are imaginary, whereas in life there are real materials that have to be manipulated if secret aspirations are to find satisfaction. Consequently, some situations in human existence belong to a real sequence of happenings, and to an ideal sequence *at one and the same time,* whence their apparent lack of logic. These situations constitute observation posts that clearly show that some facts that spring up suddenly in the course of life are no more than extremely tortuous expressions of desire. It will be seen, then, to what extent desire's implacable demand "strikingly rearranges external factors in its search for its object by egotistically exerting itself to keep only those that can serve its ends. It is hardly more to be distracted by the roar of busy streets than by the trembling of a veil. There is desire, cutting up the wholecloth of what will not change quickly enough, then sewing the pieces together with its fine strong thread. It gives ground to no objective arbiter of human conduct." It is to instinct that desire owes its prescience and finesse, and instinct attains its goals by devious routes, the nature of which scientific discoveries are little by little revealing, and upon which rest the universe's ultimate explanations.

A corroboration of this arises from the replies made to questions put by André Breton and Paul Eluard, such as "Can you say what was the most important encounter of your life? To what degree do you assign to it, or does it assign to you, an impression of fortuity? Or of necessity?"

The replies conveyed that "the present confusion derives from the compulsion of logical thought to explain factually nature's laws and aims, etc., so that they do not blend objectively with the laws and the aims, etc., as they exist in man's inner consciousness." In fact, an analysis of all the objective and subjective circumstances that make two people, quite unknown to one another, come together in a so-called fortuitous fashion shows that their mutual affinity was formulated in the depths of their subconscious in advance of the event. The aspiration toward someone who first figured in childhood imaginings or in a dream acts on an individual's conduct in such a way that he is apt suddenly to find himself in the right circumstances for realizing that aspiration. Chance, then, is no more than "the impact of an external causality and an internal finality."

Thus, André Breton, in *L'Amour Fou*, gives an account of an unexpected encounter in the neighborhood of Les Halles on May 29, 1934, with a young woman who was "*scandalously* beautiful." One evening, some days later, elated by the object of his love, he opened one of his books and chanced on a poem entitled "Tournesol," which was written in May or June, 1923, and which was like a prophetic account of the adventure. This instance confirms a statement found in *Les Vases Communicants:* "Auto-analysis can, at times, break down the content of actual happenings to the extent of showing them to depend entirely upon previous events that were not controlled by the mind in the least." Thus, the various moments of time are closely integrated, and a man's future can be read in a crystal ball, since it is contained in the present. Often, when our most careful calculations or our best-founded conjectures have gone astray, we attribute the cause to bad luck. But, on close examination, we shall find the matter foreshadowed in a past action or dream, or even, on occasion, in a clairvoyant's predictions. "When chance shows us that our limits can be infinitely extended, we regret our prudence and our cautious ways, and we are unhappy." Consequently, introspection lies at the base of freedom—the freedom of a more intense life, and one that is expressive of an integrated being.

Surrealism, then, can also be thought of as a way of attaining a better understanding of life's real goal. "A very particular conspiracy ought to be fomented around every individual, and one that does not exist only in his imagination, admitted solely from the point of view of consciously allowing for it, but one that he should express much more dangerously by putting first his head, and then an arm, between the bars in order to escape from logic, that most detestable of prisons." And Louis Aragon further confides: "I no longer want to curb the mistakes made by my fingers or the errors made by my eyes. I know now that they are not clumsy pitfalls, but channels of inquiry toward a goal that only they can reveal to me . . . glorious gardens in which grow preposterous creeds, insights, frenzies, and obsessions."

Therefore, an enlarged necessity should be conceived,

which will include both human necessity and natural necessity. We can go as far as to allow that external necessity is subject to human necessity, just as the real depends upon the Surreal. André Breton is himself attached "to nothing so much as to what precautions and ruses desire brings to its maneuvers in the waters of preconsciousness when in quest of its object—and to what means, stupefying to a new degree, it resorts in order to make its object known to the conscious mind."

Similarly, it is not "by chance" that we make one purchase rather than another. "Each of us has only to refer the matter to himself, to look at the things he likes to surround himself with, to ask himself what it was that made him buy this or that, why his attachments have undergone such eclipses, and then let him elucidate, if he can, the reasons for his affective state regarding those things." Thus, André Breton likes to stroll round the junkshops, and to discover why his attention has been caught by this or that display stall. In that way, when with Alberto Giacometti, he happened to buy a "half-mask made of metal," and later he found himself using it to complete a sculpture he had not been able to finish until then. And thus it is that we recognize in this way of seeing the *thing found,* this "wonderful precipitation of desire." In this, does it not strictly fulfill the same office as the dream, in the sense that it frees the individual from his paralyzing affective scruples, reassures him, and makes him aware that the obstacle he believed insurmountable has been overcome?

The thing found, then, acts as a catalyst, since by making the individual realize his repressed desire it relieves him from the disquiet that his unsatisfied desire has been obscurely inflicting.

This is why the disclosure of an unforeseen action's real cause produces an emotion altogether special, which André Breton describes in this way:

> At the crisis of the discovery, occupying the period between the moment when the early navigators sight land and the moment when they put foot on shore, or the period between the instant when any adept acquires self-mastery, seeing this as testimony of a phenomenon until then unknown to him, and the instant in which he starts to gauge his observation's significance—all idea of the passage of time vanishing in the intoxication of *chance*—a fine pencil-stroke of fire releases a sense of life, or perfects it, as nothing else can. It is to the re-creation of this particular state of mind that Surrealism has always aspired, disdaining in the last analysis both the substance and the shadow for what is already no longer the shadow and is still not the substance: the shadow and the substance fused in a superlative flash of lightning.

Thus, reality and Surreality interact without pause, and Surrealism's aim is to show the unity of these two worlds, seemingly so opposed. According to Rolland de Reneville, "Such research arises from the hypothesis that the phenomena of subjective representation and those of the external world are interchangeable. This results in submitting events to a method of study that has so far been applied only to mental phenomena: psychoanalysis, which thus applied, becomes an analogous key, the use of which restores a concept of man and the world that has not ceased to be shared by primitives, mystics, poets, and all those who, as Novalis said, make external objects from thoughts, and thoughts from external objects."

SURREALISM wants to develop the human personality by bringing repressed desires into consciousness. In this it differs from spiritualism, which dissociates the personality, whereas Surrealism "proposes nothing less" than to unify it. The danger of self-analysis is that of losing oneself in the process, of not knowing how to synthesize the data in a richer conception. André Breton, then, endeavors to show us that the material unearthed in such analysis should be examined in the light of consciousness. Automatism is not an end in itself; it can only serve to augment self-knowledge, and it should only be taken into account in order to modify conduct. Many authors, he writes, "are quite generally satisfied to let the pen run on over the paper without noticing in the least degree what takes place within them, although this exposition is easier to grasp and more interesting to study than either premeditated writing or an assembly of elements taken from dreams in a more or less arbitrary way, and collected together more for the sake of their picturesque patterns than for the purpose of usefully observing their workings. Such jumbles, by their nature, will, of course, deprive us of all the benefits to be gained from this kind of operation." These Surrealist inquiries should be modeled upon clinical examinations, except that the examiner and the patient are one and the same person. "In this respect, nothing is more useful than to attempt to 'follow' certain *subjects* taken from the normal world, as well as from the other, and this in a spirit that defies at once the spirit of the fortunetelling booth and that of the consulting room, and which, in a word, will be the *Surrealist* spirit. The results of these observations should, of course, be recorded in an exclusively naturalist form, and one free of all poetic tendencies."

Surrealism, although it starts by extolling a surrender to the imagination and a relaxing of the will, is far from having human resignation as its end. The sole preoccupation of its disciples should be to discover through it new perspectives. [1] Although artists are especially gifted for investigating the sphere of the subconscious, they ought not to forget that, before all else, they are experimenters, charged with disclosing to man his hidden powers. As Antonin Artaud has written, "I give myself up to the fever of my dreams, but this is in order to deduce new laws from it." Also, "If our spiritual profundities harbor strange forces capable of enhancing those of the surface, or capable of struggling victoriously against them," says André Breton, "there is every advantage in capturing them . . . and then submitting them, if there is occasion, to the control of reason."

THE SURREALISTS, then, have made a deep study of contradictions and incoherences only to secure their unity the better, thus agreeing with Jung, for whom "consciousness and the unconscious do not necessarily oppose each other; on the contrary, they complement one another, and together form a single whole: individuality," which is to be thought of as an entity superior to the conscious Ego, since it also includes the unconscious Self. This "enlarged consciousness," freed from disturbing beliefs and desires, "positively links the individual to objective reality."

André Breton lays stress on this emancipation of the human being, which alone can satisfy him fully. Once the submerged and hidden world has been explored, the matter is nothing less than one of reclaiming thought's "original purity," a decision that presupposes an immense impartiality and a no less great contempt for risk. Also, "The Surrealist operation has a chance of being carried out successfully only if it is achieved under conditions of *moral asepsis,* which is still something that very few men care to hear spoken of." Reproaches such as those which contend that Surrealism "boasts of wanting to consider what is most vile, most disheartening, and most corrupting in the world" indicate a total incomprehension of its endeavors.

To some extent these criticisms recall those that are nowadays addressed to Sartre, but the Surrealists outdistance them because they are only apologists for the unavowable, the better to give man a consciousness that he himself has ennobled. "Why are we made and what should we agree to serve? And what ought we to abandon as being beyond all hope? From this anguish is the question formed that occupies us," proclaims André Breton in *Les Pas Perdus.*

Surrealism, far from being a pessimistic concept of life, not only reveals unsuspected possibilities to man, but strives as well to furnish him with the means to realize them. That is why the Surrealists have again turned toward the real, and why they have built up a theory of social action qualified to change the external conditions that limit man's existence. They have retraced their steps from Surreality to reality, and also to politics, by a measure like that of the Platonic philosopher who, after gazing at the sun, rejoined the prisoners in the cave in order to guide them to the light.

The Social Aspect

Some people, such as Jacques Vaché, later followed by Jacques Rigaud and René Crevel, wishing to put themselves beyond the reach of a society that was not made for them, imitated Gérard de Nerval and quitted it voluntarily, by suicide. Surrealist inquiries into suicide found that one of its principal causes was the social repression of the libido. However, André Breton is far from confusing love with the tyranny of uncontrolled instincts. The secret aspiration of us all is to experience a unique love, an *Amour Fou*, according to the title of one of his works. The freeing of the desires simply serves to give the energy necessary for realizing what is most frequently no more than an ideal. All Paul Eluard's poetry also extols this single being who ends by being confounded with "a reality beyond the reach of thought and words," since the quest for unity, which links all Surrealist conduct, invests this being with the supreme aspect of love.

André Breton, faithful to his method of explaining the being's deep tendencies, analyzes the reasons why we consider it wrong that love once satisfactory should compulsively vanish. According to him, this sophism has, in the first place, a social cause, deriving from the fact that "in love, original choice is not *really* permitted, so that, in the same degree in which it exceptionally tends to impose itself, it occurs in an atmosphere of non-choice most hostile to its triumph." There are prejudices of class and background that divide individuals who were intended to unite. To surmount them is to incur social exclusion, and to submit to them is to incur a lifelong nostalgia for a glimpsed happiness.

The second cause, this time a moral one, arises from "the incapacity, which affects the great majority of men, to free their love from all fear and all doubt, and to expose themselves without defense to the dazzling gaze of their idol." It follows, then, that they should free themselves from this concept of sin, which prevents them from giving themselves wholeheartedly to a single being.

This rehabilitation of humanity's fundamental aspiration should not remain merely a mental attitude. It demands a recasting of society to allow the individual to be himself without bowing to the hypocrisies of a narrow morality. To achieve this, it is necessary "to go beyond such absurd distinctions as those made between the beautiful and the ugly, the true and the false, good and evil." Surrealism has become "a dogma of absolute rebellion, of total insubmission and of sabotage to order." It looks toward nothing less than violence.

Some books, such as Louis Aragon's *Le Libertinage*, describe life on society's fringes and show what extravagances must be resorted to by those eccentrics who do not want to compromise. Similarly, "good sense" must be shocked, the crowd must be scandalized by poems, as by pictures that seem pictures only in name, and society must be shaken from its torpor by acts that horrify it. André Breton is not afraid to write that "the simplest Surrealist act is to go down into the street with revolvers in our hands, and to fire into the crowd at random for as long as we can. . . . The justice of such an act is in no way incompatible with faith in the shining light that Surrealism seeks to shed upon our deepest recesses." One of

Louis Aragon's heroes, to urge his disciples into desperate adventures, cries:

> Your hearts are as bubbles in water, and in them I see better than you the source of your terror. You do not so much dread the unhappy outcome of a deadly adventure as you fear to commit a criminal act against all you were brought up to respect. . . . Yes, that tells me all: cruelty, felony, the names alter cases with men, and their opposites are weakness, weakness, and weakness. Only excesses deserve our enthusiasm, and if they relate only to hatred there's no doubt but that sooner or later they will gain us a more durable love.

These terroristic acts will be just so many ways of denouncing bourgeois pseudo-morality, and of leading others toward a revolution affecting the whole of existence.

SURREALISM, then, has undergone an intense evolution. At first oriented toward the mystical, it has become more positive. Psychoanalysis has made it possible to apply the concept of Surreality to the unconscious, where it can be scientifically studied. However, since the Surrealists do not wish their concept to remain a chimera accessible only to a few privileged people, they seek to deliver it from the yoke of the capitalist system by applying Karl Marx's theories. *Le Second Manifeste du Surréalisme,* which appeared as early as 1929, had a clearly political character, and in it André Breton, having deplored that "some things are, while others, which could so easily be, are not," precisely stated his aim like this: "We advance so that those two groups of things may either be intercepted singularly when the limit is reached, or become as one. The point is not to rest, but *to do no less than exert ourselves desperately up to that limit.*" The review *La Révolution Surréaliste* became, in 1930, *Le Surréalisme au Service de la Révolution,* a significant change of name if one thinks of the anarchic individualism that characterized the movement's beginnings. However, the first condition of spiritual liberation, the liberation of man, was something that could be attained only by the proletarian revolution.

From that time on there took place a revival of all the great themes of historic materialism, struggling against "a monstrous system of slavery and hunger," since "we live in open conflict with the immediate world surrounding us, an ultra-sophisticated world, a world that, in some questionable aspects, proves itself to be *without an alibi. . . .* The taint of money is over everything, and everywhere is found a dismal resignation to a huge increase in frivolities and spectacles." It is necessary to destroy all these capitalist privileges that browbeat the individual and oppress him from infancy.

The Surrealists were anxious to avoid the danger that the individualist authors had fallen into. Thus, to them, Dostoievsky's characters, by reason of their sterile analyses, degenerate into mystical romantics out of touch with reality, and so sink into the nihilism of despair.

To see in the dream only a means of evasion, and to attribute to it a supranatural role by opposing it to action, leads to the unsatisfied state that the human being finds in society as presently constituted. And for that reason, this tendency, impoverishing the individual as it does, should be fought. Man ought not to resign himself to the conditions that are given him, but should dominate them with all his regained energies.

In particular, man vitiates his energy when he returns to his past, whereas, on the other hand, he enriches it if he turns toward action. To quote René Crevel:

> Take out from the depths what man holds as holy treasures, though "unholy" would be nearer the mark in view of the mass of ignorance, neglect, and denial that stands between him and those so-called treasures; bring into the world by the appropriate measures (sleep, the transcription of dreams, automatic writing, and clearly characterized simulations of delirium) that which, beneath the thicknesses in which it has been enveloped, every creature will look upon as his noumenal nucleus; explore the unconscious as far as that remote, dark den in which man's desires huddle, stultifying themselves from fear of man-killing avalanches; trace broad, plain, lighted highways through the land that seemed once the prey of landslides; restore to common use all that was forbidden territory; design new chan-

nels of communication for those who would give a good re-
ception to bad conditions, and who draw apart, greedy for
an isolation in which they pretend to accept stupid wretch-
edness for a touching magnificence—these points of view
were also the points of juncture with Marx and Engels, for
whom the Thing in Itself (*das Ding an sich*), instead of remaining the ungraspable noumenon of Kantian philosophy,
the tabooed object lurking in the last metaphysical refuges,
ought, on the contrary, to transform itself into the Thing for
Others. In that way, from the dessicated human, Surrealism
resuscitates man.

Freudianism has extricated the individual from limited
moral conceptions, and has shown the strength of the
instincts, but the life-force thus released only transforms
human existence if the world is transformed. Surrealism,
then, has as an end the reconciling of the conflict between
action and the dream, so as to form a "method of knowledge developing within the framework of dialectical materialism, giving the word 'dialectical' the implication that
Karl Marx gave it of 'greater consciousness,'" which accords
with his psychological conception of fusion of the unconscious and consciousness.

Thus, the Surrealist movement is far from being a
contemplative philosophy, a flight beyond the real, as it
might have tended to become. From the start it has shown
that thought is common to all, and that there is a sort of
universal consciousness. Its social tendencies were pre-
figured in the attention it gave to recent scientific dis-

coveries, to machinism, and to its enveloping sense of the marvelous, but it was only later that these tendencies were concretely expressed by adherence to Marxism. "The problem that faces the Surrealists," Pierre Naville recognizes, "is to know in what conditions the mind actually lives, and, if it stifles, if it dies, what are the real conditions of its salvation. . . . Surrealism owes its reality, and its life, to what is necessary, not to the decomposition of the spirit, but to its greater development."

Thus, Surrealism "belongs to this immense enterprise of re-creating the universe to which Lautréamont and Lenin gave themselves wholly and entirely." Paul Eluard even holds Surrealism to be

> an instrument of conquest as well as defense. . . . Let man discover himself, let him know himself, and feel himself at once capable of seizing all the treasures of which he has been almost entirely deprived, of all the treasures material as well as spiritual that have been accumulating for all time at the price of the most terrible sufferings, and all for a small number of privileged persons blind and deaf to everything that constitutes human grandeur.

Moreover, in historical materialism André Breton found new arguments to justify his dialectical concept of the union of contradictions, and arrived at "a particular philosophy of inherence according to which Surreality is contained even in reality—without being either higher than it, or outside it—and, by reciprocity, the container will also be the thing contained. The concept is almost that of a *communicating vessel*[1] acting between the contained and the container." In this sense the Surreal is no more than the unknown real, and to the extent that its mystery endures, poets and philosophers will strive ardently toward its solution.

SOME CRITICS were deceived by this evolution, and Rolland de Renéville reproached André Breton for "abandoning the idealist position in favor of dialectical materialism. . . . If the Surrealists renounce the idea of leading us directly to the conquest of our nature, so that from then on it influences facts—in the broad hope that our turning to them will, by itself, bring us this victory—it is permissible to ask if this point of view does not constitute, in reality, the liquidation of a doctrine on behalf of which, by a sort of anachronism, I deliver speeches of confidence."

However, André Breton, in *Les Vases Communicants,* clearly states his exact position: "I know that this world—the external world—exists outside myself, and I have never ceased to be confident about it. I do not believe, as Fichte believed, in the non-Self created by the Self. To the extent that I get out of the way when cars go by, and do not allow myself to verify the accurate functioning of a firearm

[1] In French *un vase communicant,* referring to André Breton's book *Les Vases Communicants.*

at the cost of what seems good to me—myself, as it were—I hasten to take off my hat most gracefully to this world, and think that that should be enough." He considers, then, that it is easy for him "to show, contrary to what certain detractors insinuate, that of all the specifically intellectual movements revealed to the light of day, Surrealism is the only one that is forearmed against all inclination toward the idealist fantasy."

According to him, it was consistent with Surrealism's natural development that it should converge upon dialectical materialism. Right from the start he recognized that he supported a subjective idealism, but was opposed, nevertheless, to mechanistic materialism—the two antagonistic positions implying a duality between matter and mind that had to be resolved. Already Hegel's absolute idealism, essentially synthetical, was more satisfying, and, for the rest, it was dialectical materialism that transposed it to the plane of action. "The Surrealists, having enclosed the whole revolt in universal humor—the same fastening that Lautréamont used—sought to leave it through Marxism."

They clearly felt that logic had to be fought by showing that ambivalence is fundamental to life, and by underlining the conflicts revealed by exploration of the unconscious. However, it was not possible to cleave to these negations, and a third term had to be found that was the synthesis of this apparent opposition between the real and the Surreal. André Breton, unlike Hegel, could not find this synthesis in the Idea, which he saw as a static and reactionary notion that would result in a totalitarian state, a concept contrary to the freedom he was seeking.

Only the solution of Marx and Engels, who maintained that "excess is within the impulse of life and action," could satisfy him. And, indeed, it led to the envisaging of man as an assembly of qualities freely developing.

HEGEL constructed his philosophy only to show this paradox of the *unhappy consciousness* separated on two antithetic planes, irremediably enclosed in itself, yet nevertheless "filled with an unhappy love for the absolute." He retraces through humanity's history the stages of the Calvary that human consciousness must traverse if, in the end, it is to raise itself to the synthesis of happiness. But he was arguing from theoretical grounds, by making from man "the man with consciousness, instead of making from consciousness, the consciousness of the man, of the real man, living in a real world, objective and conditioned by himself."

Struck by this insufficiency, Kierkegaard and Marx endeavored to resolve the same problem—although by different routes—to restore to man his unity, which they envisaged from the psychological and social points of view. In thus going from earth to heaven, they were absolutely opposed to "the German philosophy that goes from heaven to earth," and they turned their backs on its idealism.

Both moved away from the antinomies of the "unhappy consciousness," the one endeavoring to reach the concept of freedom by retreating upon himself, the other making his liberation depend upon a social transformation.

The same trends of thought are found in the Surrealists' evolution. Their break with the world made them go through that agony which impelled them to question themselves, and their impotence to resolve their conflicts by themselves brought them round to seeing man largely as a social being.

Confronting this thesis presented by reality, they were driven toward its antithesis: Surreality, which is at the outset an "under-reality." The Surrealists' next task was to synthesize this antinomy. Their revolt against the insufficiencies of the real oriented them toward the mysterious, the fantastic, and the world of the dream, which they thought themselves able to grasp in its entirety. However, the better to shock routine—and pluck the masses from their torpor—they explored, above all, the realm of the terrifying and the monstrous; naturally they had all come upon the theories of Freud, who revealed to them the unassuaged instincts of the unconscious. They now abandoned metaphysics for firmer ground. But, far from being content to analyze the depths hidden beneath social and educational veneers, they saw therein the origin of the dissatisfactions suffered by the individual. Accordingly their spirit of revolt made them at once take up the Marxist theories, which held that the overthrow of prevailing social conditions would enable man to achieve a unity of self, and consequently to find true freedom. Thus, this unity of the universe, which was no more than a presentiment, finds itself confirmed by psychological analysis, and by Marxism, which has conferred upon it a positive content. The dialectical evolution of Surrealism can, then, be summed up in the names of Lautréamont, Freud, and Trotsky, each the forerunner of a particular stage.

JUST AS the revealing of the self is no more than a means leading in fact to the liberation of Surreality, so the social revolution is not an end in itself, since it is only a condition of human renewal. Above all, the revolution must redeem the human personality from the pillory of the social framework. While waiting for it to take place, the experiences of the inner life should be pursued and properly understood, independently of all "outside control, even Marxist." For there are two distinct, though complementary, problems: on the one hand, self-knowledge; on the other, social action. Moreover, constant change takes place between these two worlds, the internal and the external, "between the satisfied and the unsatisfied needs" of man, the origin of this torment, of that aspiration, and "of that spiritual thirst which from birth to death he must indispensably allay and yet not cure." As André Breton affirms: "I will not allow myself to oppose the present urgent necessity— that of changing the tottering and worm-eaten social foundations of the old world—with that other necessity, no less demanding, which is not to see the revolution as an end in itself, an end that by all the evidence could only be the same as the end of history. For me, the *end* will be no more than the knowledge of man's eternal destination, and for man in general it is only the revolution that can fully ensure that destination."

He dwells so intransigently on this point that his second interview with Jean Duché was called *Il Faut Régler Son Compte à l'Infame Précepte: La Fin Justifie les Moyens* (*It Is Necessary to Close the Account of the Infamous Precept: The End Justifies the Means*). Arthur Koestler's book *The Yogi and the Commissar* shows us the confusing perspectives of this latter point of view carried to its ultimate consequences. "This precept," adds André Breton, "is certainly one that the last free intellectuals must today oppose with the most active and categorical denial. It appears to me today that it is in this denial, made without reservations, that the true and effective affirmation of freedom resides."

Surrealism, then, cannot be thought of as a closed system, since it proclaims itself ready for incessant research, and eager to assimilate every new concept appropriate for realizing its aim. Thus its evolution can but continue.

MARXISM, far from stifling individual liberty, should provide its ideal condition, since André Breton has from the start understood it in the sense given it by Trotsky, who looked upon a totalitarian interpretation of it as treason. And for that reason Marxism can apply to a much wider field than the solution of social problems, the area to which some people would confine it. André Breton holds, as it were, "the two ends of the chain"—theory and practice—but his aspirations toward the Infinite cannot be contented with a stunted solution, since he is fully aware of the being's dynamism and its surpassing destiny. Surrealism is a complex doctrine, and its advocates feel keenly the human condition's instability. Deprived of faith and religion, they seek to disentangle this moral crisis of an unbalanced generation. Conscious of the diversity of the real, they have no wish to neglect its spiritual element in favor of an aspect solely material. Neither can they assimilate as a whole such communist concepts as those realized in Russia, since they ceaselessly desire to safeguard the rights of spiritual liberty and of subjective existence; hence the schisms that have occurred among them on purely political grounds, of which the "Aragon affair" was the most resounding.

Indeed, some texts consider Marxism as a general theory of knowledge. Marx himself violently criticized that crude and primitive communism which leveled individuals, and in consequence, lowered them. Private ownership will be abolished completely only if the desire for physical and material possession disappears, by the removal of all distinction between "mine" and "thine"—an extremely exalted concept, which sees in the suppression of human egoism a condition of its freedom. The social revolution and the human revolution are indivisible, and their harmony will lead to a transformation of reality from the economic and spiritual point of view.

It is to Marxism envisaged in this way that André Breton adheres when he writes: "Man cannot be contented solely by the satisfaction of his material appetites. In Marxism, as in everything else, certain problems arise, such as those of the dream and of love." To want to overthrow the world without taking these aspirations toward an ideal into account can only lead to checkmate. "Every error in the interpretation of man, then, involves an error in the interpretation of the universe." Therefore, we must conceive "a synthetical attitude in which both the need of transforming the world, and the need of interpreting it, are reconciled in the most complete way possible."

Thus, true communism "involves the appropriation of all that is the essence of humanity by man and for man, after which man returns it to himself insofar as he is a social being, which is to say, a human being, the return being complete and aware, and preserving all the riches previously accumulated—this communism will be naturalism achieved parallel with humanism."

André Breton, however, goes beyond this point of view of Karl Marx's when he cries: "The great curse is lifted, and it is in human love that all the power dwells for regenerating the world." Man, once he has become truly himself, will be able to "involve himself through and through," since, by virtue of his love and the loved one, he will identify himself, not only with all humanity, but with universal life. Love will ensure the resolving of antinomies, which is the object of the Surrealist pursuit. "Since it is by love alone that the highest degree of fusion between human existence and human essence is realized, it is by love alone that these two concepts are at once brought together in complete harmony and unequivocally, whereas those outside remain forever hostile and uneasy."

This optimistic prospect of a humanity reconciled with both itself and the universe achieves the unity sought by the Surrealists. "They do not hold to be incurable what Camus noted as the 'fracture' between the world and the human spirit. They are a long way from admitting that nature is necessarily hostile to man, but they infer that man has lost certain keys that he originally possessed, and that kept him in intimate communion with nature, and since then he has persisted, more and more feverishly, in trying others *that do not fit*." Science remains powerless to procure the keys for man, and it has disrupted that contact with nature that only poetry can give. André Breton goes so far as to see, in the setting-up of a new myth, a realization of this supreme accord between human emotions and the three kingdoms of nature.

THE POETS, then, are humanity's guides in its progress toward an ideal. Their inspiration enables them to overstep the limits of reason and so allows them to predict the stages of its evolution. Moreover, André Breton, agreeing with Tristan Tzara, considers art as a purely disinterested and absolutely independent activity—another reason why he could not concur with the Congress of Soviet Writers. As he declared in Mexico in 1938: "To those who would urge us to consent to art's submitting itself to a discipline we hold radically incompatible with our resources, we give a refusal from which there is no appeal."

A work that involves its author in taking up a position in such-and-such an attitude causes him to fall from the universal plane that is pre-eminently his. It puts a term to his vision, which should raise him far above his age, since the artist ought only "to reveal the powers of the spiritual life to knowledge" by "showing the collective consciousness what ought to be, and what was to be."

No one better than the poet, whose sensitivity has antennae denied to the mass of men, "will be able to overcome the depressing idea of an irreparable divorce between action and the dream. . . . At all costs he will keep in sight the two limits of the human affinity, and upon their destruction the most gainful conquests will at once fade to insignificance in comparison with this: the objective consciousness of realities and their inner development by its means, and this by virtue of individual perception on the one hand, universal perception on the other, will amount to a new order of magic." No one can effect better than can the poet the synthesis of "existence subject to the objective relationship of beings, and existence concretely escaping this relationship in a precipitate of beautiful and enduring color."

Just as the Surrealists did not lose themselves in exploring the depths of the unconscious, and managed to retain their critical sense in order to reveal the principles of their discoveries, so they did not give themselves up entirely to revolutionary action, since art, science, and revolution converge toward the same goal: the harmony of man and the universe. Ignoring the temptation of art for art's sake they had to be like militant Communists, and in this connection Jules Monnerot compared them to the Gnostics. "When the new Christians explained their doctrine the faithful no longer recognized their religion, just as the Communists have hardly been able to recognize their revolution in the 'Surrealist Revolution.' The Surrealist revolution is so much more 'beautiful' than the other. It is a 'fixed explosion,' it is 'circumstantial magic,' and it was born at the heart of poetry." The Communists can only beware of these poets, who not only refuse to submit to Communist discipline but intend to impose their views on the Communists.

Still, what do these misunderstandings matter when art, for the Surrealists, is the blazing torch that lights the road on which, overtaking psychoanalysis and the revolution, they go forward as pioneers of a free world!

Conclusion

The Surrealists, not content to see the world solely in its objective aspect, have discovered the source of inspiration that man bears within him and have expressed it through poems and pictures of incontestable poetic originality. A new aesthetic is displayed by these unexpected associations of images springing from those enchantments that enfold things and beings. While André Breton opens the way to the dream, Paul Eluard leads us toward the snowy summits. And similarly Louis Aragon's lyricism restores the mystery hidden under the solid aspect of the districts of Paris.

Surrealism may be considered a form of that impulse which, throughout the ages and in all countries, has infected those of the elite who have wanted to emancipate themselves to their limits. It opposes classical Western philosophy as well as every negative and hopeless concept of existence. It allies itself with the great advances of thought, which escape all historical classification since they aim at nothing less than to resolve the agonizing problem of our destiny.

Bibliography

Surrealist Works

Artaud, Antonin. *Oeuvres Complètes*. Tome I. Paris, 1956.

Breton, André. *L'Amour Fou*. Paris: N.R.F., 1938.

————. *Anthologie de l'Humour Noir*. Paris: Le Sagittaire, 1940.

————. *Arcane 17*. Paris: Le Sagittaire, 1947.

————. *L'Art Magique*. Paris: Club Française du Livre, 1957.

————. *La Clé des Champs*. Paris: Le Sagittaire, 1953.

————. *Entretiens*. Paris: N.R.F., 1952.

————. *Les Manifestes du Surréalisme*. . . . Paris: Le Sagittaire, 1955.

————. *Nadja*. New York: Grove, 1960.

————. *Point du Jour*. Paris: N.R.F., 1934.

————. *Position Politique du Surréalisme*. Paris: Le Sagittaire, 1935.

————. *Le Revolver à Cheveux Blancs.* Paris: Cahiers Libres, 1932.

————. "The Situation of Surrealism between the Two Wars," *Yale French Studies,* Fall–Winter, 1948.

————. *Le Surréalisme et la Peinture.* New York: Brentano's, 1945.

————. *Les Vases Communicants.* Paris: Cahiers Libres, 1932.

————, Deharme, Lise, Gracq, Julien, and Jean Tardieu. *Farouche à Quatre Feuilles.* Paris: Grasset, 1955.

————, and Paul Eluard. *L'Immaculée Conception.* Paris: Editions Surréalistes, 1930; *Notes sur la Poésie.* Paris: G.L.M., 1936.

————, Eluard, Paul, and René Char. *Ralentir Travaux.* Paris: Editions Surréalistes, 1930.

————, and Philippe Soupault. *Les Champs Magnétiques.* Paris: Au Sans-Pareil, 1921.

Crevel, René. *Le Clavecin de Diderot.* Paris: Editions Surréalistes, 1932.

Dali, Salvador. *La Conquête de l'Irrationnel.* Paris: Editions Surréalistes, 1936.

————. *La Femme Visible.* Paris: Editions Surréalistes, 1930.

Desnos, Robert. *Domaine Publique.* Paris, 1953.

————. *La Liberté ou l'Amour.* Paris: Kra, 1927.

Eluard, Paul. *Donner à Voir.* Paris: N.R.F., 1939.

————. *L'Evidence Poétique.* Paris: G.L.M., 1937.

————. *A Toute Epreuve.* Paris: Editions Surréalistes, 1930.

————. *La Vie Immédiate.* Paris: Cahiers Libres, 1932.

Ernst, Max. *La Femme 100 Têtes.* Paris: Editions Surréalistes, 1929.

Hugnet, G. *Petite Anthologie du Surréalisme*. Paris: J. Bucher, 1934.

Naville, Pierre. *La Révolution et les Intellectuels*. Paris: N.R.F., 1927.

Peret, Benjamin. *La Grand Jeu*. Paris: N.R.F., 1935.

Tzara, Tristan. *Grains et Issues*. Paris: Denoël et Steele, 1935.

Works on Surrealism

Alquié, Ferdinand. *Philosophie du Surréalisme*. Paris: Flammarion, 1955.

Balakian, Anna E. *Literary Origins of Surrealism: A New Mysticism in French Poetry*. New York: King's Crown Press, 1947.

Barr, Alfred H., Jr. (ed.). *Fantastic Art, Dada, Surrealism*. 3d ed. New York: Museum of Modern Art, 1947.

Breton, André. *What Is Surrealism?*, tr. David Gascoyne. Criterion Miscellany No. 43. London: Faber & Faber, 1943.

Calas, Nicholas. "Surrealist Intentions," *Trans/formation*, I (1950), 48–52.

Desnos, Robert. "Surréalisme," *Cahiers d'Art* (Paris), I, No. 8 (October, 1926), 210–213.

Fowlie, Wallace. *The Age of Surrealism*. Bloomington: Indiana University Press, 1960. (Paperback.)

Gascoyne, David. *A Short Survey of Surrealism*. London: Cobden-Sander, 1935.

Gauss, Charles Edward. "The Theoretical Backgrounds of Surrealism," *Journal of Aesthetics and Art Criticism*, II, No. 8 (Fall, 1943), 37–44.

Greenberg, Clement. "Surrealist Painting," *Horizon* (London), XI, No. 61 (January, 1945), 49–56.

Janis, Sidney. *Abstract of Surrealist Art in America.* New York: Reynal & Hitchcock, 1944.

Jean, Marcel. *The History of Surrealist Painting,* tr. S. W. Taylor. New York: Grove, 1960.

Josephson, Matthew. *Life Among the Surrealists.* New York: Holt, Rinehart & Winston, 1962.

Kyrou, Ado. *Surrealism in the Cinema.* Paris: Arcanes, 1953.

Lemaître, Georges. *From Cubism to Surrealism in French Literature.* Cambridge: Harvard University Press, 1941.

Marcel, Jean, and Arpad Mazei. *History of Surrealist Painting.* Paris: Editions du Seuil, 1959.

Masson, André. "Le Surréalisme et Après," *L'Oeil,* V, No. 5 (May 15, 1955), 12–17.

Nadeau, Maurice. *Histoire du Surréalisme; Documents Surréalistes.* Paris: Club des Editeurs, 1958.

Peyre, Henri. "The Significance of Surrealism," *Yale French Studies,* Fall–Winter, 1948.

Raymond, Marcel. *From Baudelaire to Surrealism.* New York: Wittenborn, Schultz, 1950.

Read, Herbert (ed.). *Surrealism.* With an Introduction by Herbert Read. New York: Harcourt, Brace, 1936.

Schmeller, Alfred. *Surrealism.* New York: Crown, n.d.

Soby, James Thrall. *After Picasso.* New York: Dodd, Mead, 1935.

Index